Emotion

Key Concepts in Philosophy

Emotion

Carolyn Price

polity

First published in 2015 by Polity Press

Polity Press
65 Bridge Street
Cambridge CB2 1UR, UK

Polity Press
350 Main Street
Malden, MA 02148, USA

ISBN-13: 978-0-7456-5635-9
ISBN-13: 978-0-7456-5636-6 (pb)

A catalogue record for this book is available from the British Library.

Library of Congress Cataloging-in-Publication Data

Price, Carolyn, 1963-
  Emotion / Carolyn Price.
    pages cm
  Includes bibliographical references and index.
  ISBN 978-0-7456-5635-9 (hardback : alk. paper) –
ISBN 978-0-7456-5636-6 (pbk. : alk. paper)   1. Emotions
(Philosophy)   2. Emotions.   I. Title.
  B815.P75 2015
  128'.37–dc23
                                    2014036702

Typeset in 10.5 on 12 pt Sabon
by Toppan Best-set Premedia Limited
Printed and bound in the United Kingdom by CPI Group (UK) Ltd, Croydon, CRO 4YY

For further information on Polity, visit our website: politybooks.com

Contents

Acknowledgements

The ideas and arguments presented in the book first began to take shape as I wrote a book on emotion for an Open University module on the philosophy of mind a decade ago. Since then I have been developing my own views on the topic through a number of articles and talks. As a result, there are many people to thank for helping me to make progress with these issues. They include numerous Open University students; my colleagues at the Open University; seminar and conference participants at several places (including the Open University, the Institut Jean Nicod in Paris, Friedrich-Alexander Universität at Erlangen-Nürnberg and the Universities of Reading, Northampton, York, Hertfordshire and Manchester); and anonymous referees for a number of journals. Their insights and criticism have been invaluable. Particular thanks should go to my colleague Derek Matravers, who kindly read and commented on a draft of the book, and to three anonymous referees for Polity whose feedback was crucial in helping me to find a workable structure and approach. I would like to thank, too, Emma Hutchinson and Pascal Porcheron at Polity for their encouragement and advice throughout the writing process, and Justin Dyer, who copy-edited the text, for his care and patience.

In certain parts of the book, the discussion is indebted to earlier publications of mine. In the first three sections of Chapter 4, my argument is based in part on my paper 'Doing without emotions' which was published in *Pacific Philosophical Quarterly* 93(3) (2012): 317–37. Certain ideas from that article also crop up, in a smaller way, in Chapters 1 and 3. In Chapter 6, I draw on my essay 'Fearing Fluffy: the content of an emotional appraisal', published in G. Macdonald and D. Papineau (eds), *Teleosemantics* (Oxford: Oxford University Press, 2006: 208–28), and also on 'The problem of emotional significance', published in *Acta Analytica* 28(2) (2013): 189–206.

Introduction

Getting Started

As I type this opening sentence, I am feeling mildly frustrated – frustrated because I am having trouble finding a good opening sentence for this book. Earlier, I was feeling anxious about a problem at work, then grateful to hear that someone had sorted it out. When I looked out of the window this morning, I was happy to see that it had snowed. None of this, I take it, is remotely surprising. As with most people, my experience of the world is frequently tinged with emotion. Much of the time, my emotional responses are not intense: often I am hardly aware of them. Only occasionally do I panic, lose my temper or jump for joy. Still, much of what happens in my daily life has at least *some* emotional significance for me: events are heartening, annoying, worrying, exciting, embarrassing and saddening by turns. And this, I assume, is true for almost everyone.

Yet, for all their familiarity, emotions present some surprisingly complex puzzles. This is partly because, as Peter Goldie (2000) has emphasized, our emotional experiences are *themselves* complex. The point can be brought home simply by describing an emotional response. Suppose that you have just made a complete fool of yourself in front of a large group of people. You are rigid with embarrassment, and you can feel yourself sweating and blushing. Your attention is fixed on your blunder: embarrassed thoughts crowd into your mind – thoughts about what you have just said and how you might repair the damage. Perhaps you suddenly remember a similarly awful moment last week or start to imagine what your audience must be thinking. Almost certainly, you have an urge to creep away. You might also be doing certain things – spluttering out a retraction, perhaps. An emotional response, then, is not just a matter of *feeling* a certain way: it can involve thinking, wanting, remembering and imagining; it can involve changes in your body and in your behaviour.

The complexity of emotion makes it a rich topic for investigation. At the same time, this complexity can make the topic hard to approach: it is difficult to know where to start. One of my aims in this opening chapter is to provide a way into the topic, by describing some different kinds of emotional response. My discussion will highlight some features of emotion that will play an important role in the chapters that follow. I shall follow this, in the final section, by setting out my plan for the book.

Emotional Responses

An Emotional Reaction

Alice is in the library, trying to understand something complicated. Her colleague Zack walks into the room: he lets the door slam loudly behind him, breaking Alice's concentration. She bristles with anger. Almost immediately, though, she notices that Zack is struggling with a pile of heavy books, and her anger fades.

Bristling with anger is an example of what I shall call an emotional *reaction*. Other examples might include a sudden stab of fear, a surge of joy or a rush of tenderness. Emotional reactions are very brief, lasting a matter of seconds. But despite their brevity, they involve several kinds of psychological and physiological change. Alice's angry reaction, for example, might include any or all of the following:

• Her attention switches to Zack and the slamming door.
• Her heart speeds up and her muscles tense.

- She frowns and clenches her fists.
- She has an urge to do something about the situation – to shout at Zack, perhaps.

Moreover, Alice's response seems to involve a particular way of experiencing or evaluating the situation: she experiences Zack's behaviour as a kind of attack or offence. When she sees Zack struggling with his pile of books, her evaluation changes, and her anger fades. This suggests that we need to add another item to the list:

- She evaluates Zack's behaviour as offensive.

Finally, these changes generate a conscious experience, which is characterized by a particular *phenomenology* or feel. The feel of anger is determined in part by the bodily feelings that it involves: for example, Alice may feel agitated and tense. On the face of it, though, the feel of anger is not wholly physiological: it is not just tense and agitated; it is focused and vengeful too.

An Emotional Episode

Emotional reactions do not always subside straight away: sometimes they develop into something else – a full-blown *episode* of emotion. Consider, for example, the following story.

Bill does not get along well with his neighbour Yolanda. The problem is Monty, Yolanda's pampered pet python: Bill hates snakes, and Yolanda is known to be careless. One sunny afternoon, as Bill is sitting in his garden, he spots Monty slithering towards him. Gripped by fear, Bill leaps up, picks up a rake, flings it at Monty and then flees into his house. He spends several agitated minutes locking windows and doors before calling the police. It is some time before he regains his composure.

Bill's initial reaction to Monty's appearance is similar to Alice's reaction to the slamming door. Clearly, Bill evaluates Monty as a threat. We might expect, too, that his attention is fixed on Monty; his heart is racing; he is pale; he wants desperately to escape; he feels tense, jumpy, and so on. But in this case, Bill's response does not end after a few seconds: it continues to develop. As his response progresses, it might come to include any or all the following:

• Thoughts, memories and images relating to snakes and the danger they pose flood into Bill's mind.
• He casts around for a way to deal with the threat.
• He does things (throws the rake, runs into the house, locks doors and windows) designed to deal with the threat.
• He is disposed to undergo further emotional reactions – for example, anger when the police fail to arrive immediately; relief when he realizes that the threat has passed.

While the shape of an emotional reaction may be relatively easy to predict, an emotional episode can evolve in all sorts of ways. How Bill's response develops, for example, will depend on his temperament, on his past experience and on how the situation unfolds.

An Extended Emotional Episode

Bill's fearful episode lasted a matter of minutes. Arguably, though, some emotional episodes extend over much longer periods. Suppose that Ceri has discovered that her boyfriend has cheated on her: she is feeling jealous and resentful. Her jealous response might extend for days, weeks or even months.

It might be objected that this is not the right way to describe Ceri's feelings: it would be more accurate to think of her jealousy as series of separate episodes, which are sparked whenever she recalls her boyfriend's infidelity (Ekman, 1994a: 16). On this view, then, Ceri is not in the grip of a single episode of emotion. Rather, she is disposed to *become* jealous whenever she thinks about her boyfriend's behaviour. In fact, I agree that this will often be the right thing to say. In some cases, though, this way of characterizing the situation misses something important. Suppose that, in her jealousy, Ceri finds it very hard to stop thinking about her boyfriend's infidelity: her thoughts are constantly drawn back to the situation. She begins to see past events in a new light and her plans for the future are on hold. In this case, her jealousy is not just a disposition to *become* jealous whenever she is reminded about the situation: rather, it is exerting an active influence on her thoughts and plans, continually drawing her attention back to what has happened. In this situation, it makes sense to think of her jealous response as a single, evolving episode, which stretches over days, weeks or months.

An Emotional Attitude

Can there be emotional responses that last even longer – for a lifetime perhaps? I am going to suggest that there can. Here is one possible example.

Dan is an environmental campaigner. He was drawn into politics some years ago, when the government made a decision to expand his local airport. Dan felt very indignant about this decision; although most of his neighbours soon turned their attention to other things, it continued to play on his mind. He joined a campaign group, went on demonstrations and put posters up in his window. As he looked further into the issue, the focus of his indignation moved away from the decision about the airport to what he regarded as a persistent lack of regard for the environment by people in power. In recent years, he has invested a significant amount of time and energy in pursuing environmental issues; he has started to think of himself as an environmental campaigner.

Dan's indignation, we might suppose, has much in common with the other emotional responses I have described: Dan evaluates the government's policies as damaging and unjust; his attention is focused on the issue; and he is motivated to do something about it. He often has indignant thoughts about the situation; and he harbours further emotional dispositions that are explained by his indignation: for example, he is disposed to feel happy should he hear that some goal of the campaign has been achieved. Moreover, his indignation plays an active role in prompting him to look out for news about environmental issues, discuss the matter with friends, and so on. However, Dan's indignation is not a transient episode of emotion that is set to fade away or be resolved after a time: rather, it has the potential to last a lifetime. Indeed, it has come to constitute a significant theme in his life, helping to shape his friendships, interests, values, and even his sense of who he is. In what follows, I shall refer to this kind of enduring emotional response as an emotional *attitude*.

Novels and films provide plenty of examples of enduring emotional attitudes. The most striking tend to be cases of obsessive and damaging emotion: we might think, for example, of Captain Ahab's obsessive rage in Melville's *Moby-Dick*, or Miss Havisham's life-long grief and resentment in Dickens's *Great Expectations*. But it is not hard to think of less disturbing examples. In particular, love seems to be an emotion that is characteristically experienced as an emotional attitude, rather than a transient episode.[1] Novels and films provide plenty of examples of that too.

Emotional Responses: Complex, Diverse and Coherent

What can we learn from these stories? I shall suggest that they point to three key features of emotion.

(a) *Complexity*. All these stories confirm the point that I made at the start of this chapter: emotional responses are characteristically complex responses, which involve a mix of psychological, physiological and behavioural changes. As we have seen, the longer an emotional response lasts, the more complex it can become.

(b) *Diversity*. Emotional responses are not all of a kind. Most obviously, perhaps, there are different *types* of emotion: in this discussion, I have already mentioned embarrassment, anger, fear, jealousy, indignation, resentment, grief and love. It would not be difficult to come up with a much longer list. Arguably, we can also distinguish between different *classes* of emotion: for example, theorists of emotion sometimes distinguish between *moral* emotions (e.g. indignation, remorse), *intellectual* emotions (e.g. interest, wonder) and *personal* emotions (e.g. anxiety, sorrow, joy). Finally, emotional responses come in different shapes and sizes. As we have already seen, there can be momentary emotional reactions, full-blown emotional episodes and enduring emotional attitudes. In all these senses, then, emotional responses are interestingly diverse.

It is important to bear this diversity in mind in what follows: in examining any general claim about emotion – including, of course, the ones in this book – it is always worth asking whether it is true of *all* kinds of emotional response, or whether it fits certain kinds of response better than others.

(c) *Coherence*. The third point is more controversial. On the face of it, an emotional response is not just a random assortment of symptoms: it has a coherent structure. Consider, for example, Bill's fearful response to Monty. Having recognized Monty as a threat, Bill's attention is focused on the danger; he is strongly motivated to try to get away; he undergoes physiological changes that prepare him for vigorous action; he cries out and looks frightened – behaviour which might alert others to his situation. Described in this way, Bill's response has every appearance of being a co-ordinated, organized response to danger – one that might give him a chance of escaping unhurt.

It is important to be careful here. I am not suggesting that Bill's fearful response is the *most* effective response he could have produced. Perhaps it would have been better to have calmly backed away. Indeed, it is possible that, on this occasion, responding with fear made things worse. Nor have I said that Bill's response was one that he would have endorsed himself: perhaps he felt rather embarrassed after the event. I am claiming only that his fearful episode *makes sense* viewed as aimed at a certain objective – that is, dealing with a physical threat.

The same point applies to the other emotional responses described here. Alice's angry reaction, for example, makes sense as an aggressive response to offence: in her anger, she is motivated to retaliate; she is physically prepared for action; her facial expression and posture make her intentions clear. Again, this is not to say that anger is always (or ever) the best response to offence. Nor does it imply that Alice believed that it was a good response to the situation. The point is just that her reaction looks very much like an organized response to offence, not just a meaningless convulsion. As we shall see later on, there are several ways in which we might try to explain the coherence of emotion. Indeed, this will be an important issue in what follows.

The complexity and diversity claims will also have significant roles to play. In fact, there is one sense in which they are already playing a role in my discussion. These features present a challenge for any would-be theorist of emotion. The problem is that there are very few things to be said about emotion that are true in every case: complications and qualifications are always in the offing. At most, we can make some claims about what is *characteristically* so. In other words, we can make claims about what is *very often* true – and, more importantly, what is true in central or paradigm cases.

The Plan

This is a short book, and I shall need to be selective. I shall be selective, first, about the *types* of emotion that I shall discuss. I shall focus on what I shall call *personal* emotional responses – that is, responses that are plausibly viewed as relating to the subject's own personal concerns. Fear, anxiety, joy, sorrow, gratitude, jealousy, envy, embarrassment, disgust, love, regret, hope and some cases of anger, shame and pride are all plausibly viewed as emotions of this kind.

As I suggested earlier, personal emotions, in this sense, might be contrasted with moral and intellectual emotions. Admittedly, the boundaries between these categories are not clear-cut. In particular, many types of emotion can occur in both moral and personal contexts. One example is shame: someone might feel ashamed of their unkindness (a moral response); or they might feel ashamed of their lack of sporting prowess (a personal one). Indeed, a shamed response might itself involve a mix of moral and personal shame; and these feelings may be very hard to disentangle. Still, even if it is not always easy in practice to distinguish these different classes of response, there does seem to be a distinction here. (I shall say more about it in Chapter 6.)

I shall also be highly selective in the *questions* that I shall address. I shall have nothing to say, for example, about the relationship between emotion and morality. That is a very important topic, but it requires a book of its own. Nor shall I address the role of emotion in scientific inquiry; in art, music and literature; or in political life – though these are all important and interesting topics. My primary focus will be the nature of emotions and emotional evaluations, and on some of the different ways in which our emotional responses can be assessed – as fitting or misplaced; rational or irrational; authentic or inauthentic; sentimental or clear-eyed. In exploring these questions, I hope to get a better sense of the role that emotions play in our personal lives.

I shall begin, in Chapter 2, by discussing some existing accounts of emotion. My aim is not to provide a survey of the philosophical literature on emotion. Rather, I shall focus primarily on four theorists. I shall begin with the psychologist and philosopher William James (1890). James's theory of emotion emphasized both the bodily aspects of emotion and its phenomenology. In contrast, Robert Solomon (1993 [1976]) stressed the idea that emotion involves *evaluation*: to understand our emotions, he thought, we need to focus not on how the subject feels, but on how they take the world to be. I shall end by discussing accounts developed by Peter Goldie (2000) and Jesse Prinz (2004), theorists who set out to accommodate both the phenomenal and the evaluative aspects of emotion. As we shall see, though, they do this in very different ways.

In exploring these views, I hope to provide some background to the discussions that follow. I shall also try to draw out some key questions about emotion:

- What is an emotion?
- What is an emotional evaluation?
- How can we explain why people's emotional responses take the form that they do?

All these questions will be explored in the chapters that follow.

In Chapter 3, I shall begin to develop my own positive account. The chapter focuses on the third of the questions above. This might look like a rather odd way to start my account: it might seem more sensible to begin by deciding what an emotion is. But I want to start with this third question because doing so will allow me to introduce a particular theoretical approach to emotion – one that will play a crucial role throughout the book. I want to suggest that one good way to explain the structure of an emotional response is by appealing to its function – the job that it is supposed to do. The notion of a function, I shall suggest, is a historical one: the functions of our emotional responses are rooted in the past – in our evolutionary history, our cultural background and our personal experience. As I shall make clear, I do not think that this is the only productive way to think about emotion. But as we shall see, this historical, functional approach can help us to answer some important questions about emotional responses and the situations that elicit them.

With this theoretical claim in place, we will now be ready to consider what an emotion actually is. This is the topic of Chapter 4. As I shall explain, the question is ambiguous: in asking it, we might want to know what constitutes a particular *instance* of emotion – Bill's fear or Ceri's jealousy, for example; alternatively, we might want to know how to distinguish *types* of emotion (fear, jealousy) from other psychological phenomena or from each other. I shall give some attention to all these questions. But it is the first that will claim most of my attention. In fact, I want to raise the possibility that there is no good way to answer this question. This is not because it is a bad question, but because the particular nature of emotion – as complex, diverse and functionally coherent – makes it very hard to decide on an answer. In contrast, I shall offer a positive account of how we might distinguish between different types of emotion. We can do this, I shall argue, by appealing to their functional and structural properties.

The three chapters that follow are all concerned, in different ways, with emotional evaluations. In fact, as I shall explain in Chapter 5, it might be thought that emotional responses involve several different kinds of intentional state, any of which might reasonably be described as an emotional evaluation. In these chapters, I shall focus particularly on the intentional states that *initiate* emotional responses. In Chapter 5, I shall investigate what kind of states these are. It might be suggested that we should take these states to be judgements. However, an alternative view is that would do better to view them as a kind of perception, or, at least, as very like perceptions. I am going to argue against the judgement view. Indeed, I shall endorse the view that these intentional states have a number of features in common with perceptions. I shall end, however, on a cautious note: on the face of it, it is also possible to draw some contrasts between these intentional states and perceptions. This is an issue that I shall take up again in Chapter 7.

Chapter 6 is concerned with the content or meaning of these intentional states. What do they *say* about the situation? In the first part of the chapter, I shall explore some ways in which the content of these states might be thought to reflect the particular structure and function of the responses that they initiate. In the second, I shall explore a specific question about our personal emotions. I suggested earlier that these responses reflect the subject's own concerns. But how should we understand this claim? Are these responses concerned with our well-being? Or do they reflect our preferences – our values, desires or likes? As we shall see, this question is not easy to answer. One possibility is that these emotional responses reflect our *likes and dislikes*: I shall try to explain why I find this suggestion plausible, at least for a large class of emotional responses.

In Chapter 7, I shall explore some questions about the rationality of emotion. Do we have reasons for feeling as we do? When emotion and judgement conflict with each other, why do we often describe the subject's emotion as irrational? Should cases of conflicting or ambivalent emotion be described as irrational too? I shall argue that consideration of these questions draws our attention to an interesting contrast between emotion and perception. But it also highlights some further contrasts between emotion and judgement. In some respects, emotion can be seen as occupying a position midway between judgement and perception.

The questions considered in Chapters 6 and 7 bear on a broader issue about the role of emotion in our personal lives. When our emotions conflict with our reasoned beliefs, should our emotional response be disregarded, or might our emotional responses sometimes have something important and distinctive to tell us about the situation? In Chapter 7, I shall consider this question.

Finally, in Chapter 8, I shall consider two other ways in which emotional responses can be assessed. What does it mean to say that an emotional response is inauthentic or sentimental? I shall explore how these notions relate to other ways of assessing emotional responses as fitting or rational. I shall also consider the moral dimension of these phenomena: is our capacity to manufacture inauthentic and sentimental responses a morally dangerous one?

Further Reading

For an introductory book on the philosophy of emotion, see Deonna and Teroni (2012). Goldie (2010) contains an extensive collective of papers on the philosophy of emotion, giving an excellent overview of current debate, as well as some insights into the history of the topic. Solomon (2003d) is a collection of readings from Aristotle to the present day. For chapter-length surveys of the contemporary debate, you might try Goldie (2007), Deigh (2010) or de Sousa's (2014) entry in *The Stanford Encyclopedia of Philosophy*.

1

Four Theories of Emotion

Introduction

In this chapter, I shall compare and contrast some existing accounts of emotion. I am not going to try to present a comprehensive survey of the field: that would be a mammoth task. Rather, I shall focus on just four accounts (with a very brief nod to a fifth). The accounts that I have chosen represent some key positions in the philosophy of emotion, and they have played a crucial role in shaping the current debate. In investigating these accounts, I shall try to draw out some particular points of comparison and contrast. This will enable me to flag up some fundamental questions that have helped to drive the philosophical debate about emotion – questions that I shall pursue in the chapters that follow. It will allow me, too, to provide some background to the discussions later in the book, helping to put them in a broader context. As I go, I shall flag up some objections that have been raised to the accounts that I describe; but detailed critical discussion is a task for later chapters.

I shall begin with the philosopher and psychologist William James. James's account, developed at the end of the nineteenth century, has played a pivotal role in the history of the topic: many of the theories that followed can be seen as reacting in one way or another to his views. I shall then move on to consider the views of three more recent theorists: Robert

Solomon, Peter Goldie and Jesse Prinz; I shall also make very brief reference to the views of the psychologist Paul Ekman.

William James: Emotions as Bodily Feelings

James's Hypothesis

In 1890, James published *The Principles of Psychology*. The book included a bold new thesis about the nature of emotion.[1] James does not simply assert his thesis: rather, he presents it as a *hypothesis*, standing in need of empirical confirmation. He begins by focusing on what he calls the 'coarser' emotions. These are emotions that nearly everyone believes involve bodily changes. They include, he says, fear, rage, grief and love:

> Our natural way of thinking about these coarser emotions is that the mental perception of some fact excites the mental affection called the emotion, and that this latter state of mind gives rise to the bodily expression. My theory, on the contrary, is that *the bodily changes follow directly the perception of the exciting fact, and that our feeling of the same changes as they occur is the emotion.* (James, 1890: 449–50, italics in the original)

To understand what James means, it helps to think about a particular case. Consider Alice's angry reaction to the slamming door, described in Chapter 1. Hearing the door slam causes Alice to undergo certain bodily changes: her heart speeds up, her muscles tense; she frowns and clenches her fists. These bodily changes, in turn, produce certain bodily feelings: Alice feels tense and agitated. But where in this sequence of events is Alice's anger to be found? According to James, we naturally suppose that Alice's anger sits between her hearing the door slam and the bodily and behavioural changes that follow: the slamming door causes Alice's anger; and her anger, in turn, causes her to tense up and frown. James thinks that this gets things the wrong way round. The true order of events is this: the slamming door causes Alice to tense up and frown; and these bodily changes, in turn, cause Alice's anger. This is because, in James's view, Alice's anger consists of the feelings produced by the bodily changes. Hence her anger is the *effect*, not the cause, of those bodily changes.

Although James begins by making this claim specifically about the coarser emotions, it soon becomes clear that he thinks it is true of the 'subtler' emotions too. These include, for example, wonder or admiration at the aesthetic qualities of a work of art, at the intellectual qualities of a mathematical proof, or at the moral qualities of another person. In these cases, also, James thinks, 'the bodily sounding board is at work' (James, 1890: 471). According to James, then, an emotion is essentially a feeling; and, in particular, it is a bodily feeling. On this view, anger, fear, grief and love can be compared with other types of bodily feeling, such as pain, nausea, drowsiness or hunger. These bodily feelings, he thinks, are not bare sensations, devoid of meaning: rather they are ways in which we perceive or become aware of changes that are happening in our bodies.

The Causes of Emotion: Bodily Changes

What kinds of bodily change give rise to emotions, according to James? They include internal, physiological changes – for example, the quickening of the pulse and tensing of the muscles. But James also refers to various kinds of expressive behaviour: blushes, tears, flared nostrils and gritted teeth. In describing rage, he mentions what seems to be a motivational change – an impulse to violent action. This diversity, he thinks, helps to explain the extraordinary richness and subtlety of emotional experience (James, 1890: 450–2).

These bodily changes, James holds, are typically instinctive, automatic reactions to a particular type of situation or event – like blinking in sunlight or flinching at a loud noise. This is not to say, though, that our bodily responses to changes in our environment are necessarily innate or hardwired. How an individual reacts to a particular situation, he suggests, depends on a range of factors, including their personal history. When a walker meets a bear in the wood, 'fight or flight' is likely to be the default reaction; but someone who is familiar with bears might well react quite differently – with curiosity and pleasure. The walker's emotional response, James says, is a response not just to the bear, but to the total situation; and this includes their past experiences (James, 1884: 454, 518).

Nor does James hold that these bodily changes are wholly outside our control. Just as we can put off blinking or hold our breath, we can control the bodily changes that generate our emotions. This is significant, he thinks, because it means that we are able to control our emotions too. Admittedly, James's theory implies that we have no *direct* control over our emotions: once Alice's heart is racing, her teeth are clenched, and so on, she cannot help feeling these changes, any more than she can help feeling pain if she cuts her hand. Nevertheless, James thinks, she can still try to overcome her anger by controlling the changes that are happening in her body: by making an effort to relax, to breathe more slowly and to smile, she can cause herself to feel more relaxed and friendly. Conversely, she might deliberately stoke up her anger by exaggerating her angry frown and posture, by shouting or shaking the desk (James, 1890: 462–3). On James's account, then, we can control our emotions *indirectly* – by controlling the bodily changes that cause them.

James's Argument

As we have seen, James gives pride of place to emotion's *phenomenology* – how it feels. He emphasizes, too, the role of the body in generating emotional experience. This is not to say that he *locates* emotions in the body. Emotions, for James, are not bodily changes, but bodily feelings, and these are psychological states. Nor does he think that emotions are simply 'gut feelings': they are generated by a range of physiological and behavioural changes, which produce a rich and subtle range of emotional experience.

Why, though, does James think that this is the right view to take? His argument relies on the claim that feeling is what is *essential* to emotion:

> If we fancy some strong emotion, and then try to abstract
> from our consciousness of it all the feelings of its bodily

symptoms, we find we have nothing left behind, no 'mind stuff' out of which the emotion can be constituted, and that a cold and neutral state of intellectual perception is all that remains.... What kind of an emotion of fear would be left if the feeling neither of quickened heart-beats nor of shallow breathing, neither of trembling lips nor of weakened limbs, neither of gooseflesh, nor of visceral stirrings, were present, it is quite impossible for me to think.... In like manner of grief: what would it be without its tears, its sobs, its suffocation of the heart, its pang in the breastbone? A feelingless cognition that something is deplorable and nothing more. (James, 1890: 452, italics in the original)

Exactly the same point, James thinks, can be made about the 'subtler' emotional responses:

[U]nless we actually laugh at the neatness of the demonstration or witticism; unless we actually thrill at the case of justice or tingle at the act of magnanimity; our state of mind can hardly be called emotional at all. It is in fact a mere intellectual perception of how certain things are to be called – neat, right, witty, generous and the like. (James, 1890: 471)

Without feeling, James thinks, there would *be* no emotion, but only a dispassionate thought or judgement of some kind. And this, he thinks, is reason enough to conclude that the emotion *is* the feeling.

Some Worries for James

There are several kinds of objection that might be raised to James's view. First, it is important to remember that he presents his account as an empirical hypothesis, which might be disproved by scientific evidence. Indeed, he mentions a possible counter-example: he describes the case of a young man with almost no feeling in his body who was, nonetheless, reported to have exhibited a range of emotions, including anger, fear, grief and shame. James comments that cases of this kind are hard to interpret, and require further investigation (James, 1890: 455–6). More recently, Jesse Prinz (2004: 57–8) has reviewed the empirical evidence on this issue: the evidence, he reports, remains contradictory and hard to evaluate.[2]

obj

But there is scope, too, to raise some philosophical objections to James's theory. First, it is possible to question his account of the phenomenology of emotion. As we have seen, James focuses wholly on *bodily* feelings. Admittedly, he takes these to depend on a variety of phenomena, including changes in behaviour and motivation. But even so, it might well be objected that his account of emotional phenomenology is unduly restrictive (cf. Sabini and Silver, 2005; Solomon, 2007: 232–44). Consider, for example, Bill's fearful response to Monty. As well as the bodily changes described by James, this involves various psychological changes: his attention is riveted on Monty; his thoughts seem to race, as memories and images crowd into his mind; particular features of the scene may well jump out as particularly salient, influencing how things look and sound. Arguably, these psychological changes also help to determine what it feels like to be afraid.

Secondly, it might be objected that James puts too much emphasis on the phenomenology of emotion; and that, as a result, he neglects another important property of emotion: its *intentionality*. Robert Solomon, in particular, has pressed this objection to James. To say that a psychological state is intentional, in the sense that Solomon means, is to say that it is about something or directed towards something. When I think about a friend in hospital, for example, I am thinking *about* my friend. When I want a banana, I have a desire *for* a banana; when I imagine a piranha, I summon up an image *of* a piranha. In most cases, at least, intentional states also represent the object, event or situation in a particular way. When I think of my friend, for example, I think of him as sitting in hospital – as bored, perhaps, and needing a visit. When I imagine the piranha, I imagine it as baleful and toothy. Thoughts, beliefs, judgements, desires, wishes, intentions, perceptions and imaginings all seem to be varieties of intentional state.

Emotions also seem to be intentional phenomena. When Alice bristles with anger, she is not just angry: she is angry about Zack's behaviour. Moreover, to say that she is angry implies that she represents Zack's behaviour in a particular way – as offensive. The same applies in other cases too. When Bill sees Monty slithering towards him in the garden, he is not just afraid: he is afraid *of* Monty; he represents Monty as a threat. Ceri is not just jealous: her jealousy is directed *at* her boyfriend; she represents him as unfaithful. James, Solomon holds, ignores this crucial feature of emotion (Solomon, 1993 [1976]: 125–32; 2003a [1988]: 92–4; 2007: 204–5).

Is that fair? There are two points that might be made here. First, James does hold that emotions are intentional states: on his account, emotions are perceptions *of* bodily changes. This first point, though, does nothing to address Solomon's worry. Solomon's point is not simply that emotions are intentional states, but that they are directed towards objects and situations in the subject's environment: Bill's fear, for example, is directed towards Monty, out there in the garden. Secondly, and more promisingly, James holds that emotions are generally *caused* by thoughts or perceptions of things in our environment: seeing a bear, he says, causes me to fear it; remembering a dead friend causes me to feel sad; imagining her child causes a mother to experience a rush of love (James, 1890: 442–3, 450, 458). Saying that Bill is afraid of Monty, it might be suggested, is just shorthand for the claim that his feelings of fear are caused by seeing Monty.[3] It is notable, though, that we are not inclined to employ the same kind of shortcut in other, apparently similar cases. Suppose, for example, that I smell a rotten egg, and this causes me to feel sick. We would not naturally say that I feel sick about the egg: I just feel sick. We might wonder, then, whether James is able to provide an adequate account of emotional intentionality.

Robert Solomon: Emotions as Judgements

Solomon's Two Claims

What does Solomon take emotions to be? As we shall see, his views evolved over the years, but his initial suggestion is quite simple. Emotions, he argued, are not bodily feelings. Rather they are *judgements* of a certain kind: Alice's anger, perhaps, is a judgement that Zack's behaviour is offensive; Bill's fear is a judgement that Monty poses as threat; Ceri's jealousy is a judgement that her boyfriend is unfaithful (Solomon, 1993 [1976]: 125). In fact, there are two distinct claims here:

- a claim about what an *emotion* is: an emotion, Solomon thinks, is identical with the subject's emotional evaluation of the situation;
- a particular account of what an *emotional evaluation* is: an emotional evaluation Solomon suggests, is a kind of judgement.

I shall examine these two claims in turn.

'Emotions are emotional evaluations'

It is the first claim – the claim that emotions are evaluations – that allows Solomon to explain the intentionality of emotion. Emotional evaluations are undeniably intentional states: if Bill evaluates Monty as posing a threat, then his evaluation is about Monty; and it represents Monty in a certain way – that is, as posing a threat. So if emotions just *are* evaluations, emotions will be intentional states.

Does this proposal improve on James's account? There are two worries that might be raised here. First, the claim that emotions are evaluations implies not just that emotions are sometimes or often intentional phenomena, but that they *always* are. This, though, is open to question. Arguably, people sometimes experience 'objectless emotions' – emotions that are about nothing at all. In his discussion, James describes the case of a friend who suffered from bouts of objectless anxiety or panic (James, 1890: 459). We might think too of cases of emotional contagion. Suppose, for example, you find yourself surrounded by a crowd of laughing, happy people: you may find that you too are feeling happy, even though there is nothing that you are happy about. Are these cases of objectless emotion? In defence of Solomon's view, it might be suggested that these are not genuine cases of emotion at all, but rather cases of agitation or excitement. Alternatively, it might be argued that apparently 'objectless' emotions do involve an evaluation of some kind. Peter Goldie suggests that in cases of 'objectless' dread, *everything* strikes the subject as dreadful (Goldie, 2000: 17–18; see also Solomon, 1973: 21). This is not, then, a decisive objection to Solomon's claim.

The second objection is more serious. Solomon, as we have seen, argues that James's emphasis on the phenomenology of emotion leads him to neglect its intentionality. It is tempting to suggest, though, that Solomon has exactly the opposite problem: his emphasis on the intentionality of emotion leads him to neglect its phenomenology. Part of the problem, at least, arises from the fact that Solomon identifies emotions specifically with *judgements*. Some theorists hold that judgements have no phenomenal properties at all: there is nothing that it feels like to judge that Monty is a threat.[4] Even if this is wrong, though, judgements certainly do not appear to have a *bodily* phenomenology, as emotions often do.

In his early writings, Solomon denied that bodily feelings are essential to emotion. It is true, he allowed, that emotions are typically *associated with* bodily feelings, but these, he argued, are merely accompaniments or effects of emotion (Solomon, 1993 [1976]: 96–9). Later, however, he took a more concessive view. An emotion, he suggested, may well turn out to be a *combination* of judgement and bodily feelings (Solomon, 2003a [1988]: 94–5; 2003b: 189).

Indeed, Solomon's later writings contain a more radical suggestion: that the bodily feelings involved in emotion might *themselves* be regarded as a species of judgement. He calls these 'judgements of the body' (Solomon, 2003b: 191–2). To make sense of this idea, we need to start with the idea that the bodily changes involved in an emotional response are designed to help the subject to deal with the situation. Bill's fearful response, for example, involves physiological changes that prepare his body for flight, and perhaps, too, an instinctive shrinking away from the approaching threat. In sensing these bodily changes, then, Bill becomes aware of the situation as one that he is already engaged with in a particular way – one that he is already preparing to flee. Hence, these bodily feelings might be viewed as offering a kind of *verdict* on the situation, a verdict that echoes Bill's (non-bodily) judgement that he is in danger.

Solomon's final suggestion, then, is not that Bill's fear is a combination of evaluation and feeling, but, rather, that it is a cluster of evaluations, one of which may well be a 'judgement of the body'. This raises a number of questions. Here, though, I just want to highlight what Solomon is trying to achieve by making this claim. Rather than treating intentionality and phenomenology as two distinct aspects of emotion, Solomon is attempting to forge a connection between them. He does this by trying to establish that being aware of changes in one's body can itself constitute a way of recognizing the situation as having a certain kind of significance (as being threatening, say). We shall come across some other, similar suggestions later in this chapter.

'Emotional evaluations are judgements'

When Solomon says that emotional evaluations are judgements, what does he mean? In his paper 'On Emotions as Judgments' (2003a [1988]), Solomon sets out eleven characteristics of emotional judgements. Here, I shall highlight six that will be particularly relevant in what follows.

(1) *A judgement is an action.* A judgement, Solomon says, is an *act* of judging: it is the act of *forming* a belief, not the state of believing that results. He does not wish to deny, though, that there can be long-term, extended emotions: judging, he suggests, is not always a momentary act; it can be a continuing activity. Consider, for example, Ceri's jealousy. On Solomon's view, it is not that Ceri judges, once and for all, that her boyfriend is unfaithful. Rather, she is continually *renewing* her judgement: she makes it again and again, as the situation develops. Moreover, Solomon thinks, forming a judgement is not something that merely happens to her: it is something she actively does, and over which she is able to exercise a degree of direct control (Solomon, 2003a [1988]: 110–13; 2003c: 210–16).

(2) *Emotional judgements are systematic.* An emotion, Solomon suggests, is not a single, isolated judgement: 'That was offensive!' or 'He's cheating on me!' Rather, an emotion involves a complex *system* of judgements:

> [A]nger is not just a judgment of offense but a network of interlocking judgments concerning one's status and relationship with the offending party, the gravity and mitigating circumstances of the offense and the urgency of revenge. Love is not just the admiration of the other's virtues but a system of judgments about shared identities and interests, personal looks, charms, status and mutual concerns. (Solomon, 2003a [1988]: 101)

Moreover, these judgements make sense only when viewed against the background of the subject's existing beliefs, desires and past experiences. So, although it is often convenient to say 'anger is a judgement of offence' or 'fear is a judgement of danger', we should remember that this is a simplification: according to Solomon, emotional judgements are *sets* of judgements, which presuppose certain ways of thinking about and engaging with the world.

(3) *Emotional judgements are spontaneous.* Emotional judgements, Solomon argues, are not usually the result of deliberation or reasoning. Rather, they are immediate, spontaneous responses. In this respect, he suggests, they can be compared to perceptual judgements. Suppose, for example, that you feel your chair suddenly wobble beneath you. In this case, you do not stop to reflect on your perceptual experience to decide what it implies: as soon as you feel the chair move, you judge that it is unstable. In most cases, Solomon suggests, emotional judgements are spontaneous in just this sense (Solomon, 2003a [1988]: 96–7).

(4) *Emotional judgements are evaluative judgements.* Emotional judgements, Solomon thinks, are not simply judgements of fact: rather, they are evaluative or normative judgements. When someone grieves for a dead friend, for example, they do not simply register the fact that their friend has died. Rather, they represent the death as something *bad* – as a terrible loss. Similarly, when someone feels happy at the prospect of a holiday, they do not simply register that the holiday is approaching. Rather, they represent the holiday as something *good* – as something that they will enjoy (Solomon, 2003a [1988]: 99–100).

(5) *Emotional judgements are self-involved.* To respond emotionally to a situation, Solomon suggests, is in part a matter of taking it *personally*: we take it to have a particular kind of significance *for ourselves*. This is not to say that emotional judgements are always *about* ourselves. It is possible, for example, to be indignant on someone else's behalf or to feel sad about something that has happened to someone else. But even in these cases, he thinks, one judges the situation as having some kind of personal significance (Solomon, 2003a [1988]: 103–4; cf. Prinz, 2004: 62–4).

(6) *Emotional judgements are essentially tied to desires.* On the one hand, Solomon argues, certain kinds of emotional judgement *presuppose* certain kinds of desire. We cannot

make sense of Ceri's jealousy, for example, unless we assume that, at some level, she still wants her boyfriend's love and attention (or at least, that she wants nobody else to have it). On the other hand, certain kinds of emotional judgement dictate certain kinds of action: they are judgements about what kind of behaviour is called for by the situation – retaliation or celebration, say (Solomon, 2003a [1988]: 105–8).

We might wonder, then, why Solomon does not go a step further and allow that emotions include desires as well as judgements. The reason seems to be something like this. Consider Alice's anger with Zack: according to Solomon, her anger implies that she judges that his behaviour is offensive. This judgement, Solomon thinks, presupposes a particular way of conceiving the situation – a conception on which an inconsiderate act calls for retaliation. Hence, in understanding how Alice judges the situation to be, we already know what kind of action she is ready to take. We do not need to add 'and she wants to retaliate'. As I understand it, then, Solomon's point is that desires are not a *distinct* or *additional* component of emotion: they are inseparably bound up with the subject's judgements.

Solomon's account of the nature of emotional evaluations is complex and subtle. Nevertheless, it is open to question. As we saw earlier, there are many kinds of intentional state. It would be perfectly possible, then, to agree that emotions are (or typically involve) emotional evaluations without supposing that emotional evaluations are judgements. It might turn out that they are beliefs, or desires, or perceptions, or something else altogether. As we shall see, Goldie and Prinz offer rather different accounts of what emotional evaluations are.

James and Solomon: Contrast and Comparison

There are some easy contrasts to be drawn between James's and Solomon's accounts, especially if we focus on Solomon's earlier writings. For James, what matters about emotion is its phenomenology; and this, he thinks, is primarily bodily phenomenology. For Solomon, in contrast, the crucial feature of emotion is its intentionality. As a result, James and Solomon disagree about what emotions *are*. According to James, an emotion is a set of bodily feelings. According to Solomon, an emotion is a set of judgements that represent the situation in a particular way.

Moreover, the two accounts offer different views of the role that emotions play in our psychological lives. For James, emotions are primarily brief occurrences, generated by automatic bodily responses to particular kinds of situation. We can control them, he thinks, but only indirectly – for example, by controlling our posture and facial expression. Solomon, in contrast, emphasizes the interconnections between our emotions and our other psychological states. For him, our emotions reflect our existing beliefs and values; they are ways of *interpreting* the situation. They can be brief, but they can be lasting too. Moreover, for Solomon, forming a judgement is something that we *do*: hence, an emotion is not a passive response but a mental act.

There is, though, one issue on which these two theorists agree. In the previous chapter, I emphasized that an emotional response, taken as a whole, is typically a complex event, involving bodily changes, feelings, thoughts, desires, and so on. Neither Solomon nor James dispute this. Nevertheless, they both draw a distinction between an emotional response taken as a whole and the emotion itself. The emotion, they think, is a particular component of the emotional response – the bodily feeling, or the emotional evaluation.

When we take account of Solomon's later writings, however, the picture gets more complicated. As we have seen, Solomon comes to accept that feeling, as well as judgement, may be essential to emotion. Moreover, although he continues to emphasize the role of judgement in emotion, he increasingly emphasizes the complexity of emotional responses. He does this by stressing the links between emotional judgements, feelings, desires and actions.

Peter Goldie: Emotions as Complex Processes

'Complex, Episodic, Dynamic and Structured'

In his book *The Emotions*, published in 2000, Peter Goldie takes up this theme of the complexity of emotion. As we shall see, though, he develops it in a rather different way. In the opening pages of his book, Goldie summarizes his account as follows:

> An emotion – for example, John's being angry or Jane's being in love – is typically complex, episodic, dynamic and structured. An emotion is complex in that it will typically involve many different elements: it includes episodes of emotional experience, including perceptions, thoughts and feelings of various kinds, and bodily changes of various kinds; and it involves dispositions, including dispositions to experience further emotional episodes, to have further thoughts and feelings, and to behave in certain ways. Emotions are episodic and dynamic, in that, over time, the elements can come and go, and wax and wane, depending on all sorts of factors, including the way in which the episodes and dispositions interweave and interact with each other and with other aspects of the person's life. And an emotion is structured in that it constitutes part of a narrative – roughly, an unfolding sequence of actions and events, thoughts and feelings – in which the emotion itself is embedded. (Goldie, 2000: 12–13)

What is an emotion? In answering this question, as we have seen, James and Solomon each single out a particular *component* of an emotional response – the component that they take to be essential or fundamental to emotion. Goldie, in contrast, takes a much more inclusive approach. According to him, the emotion is pretty much the *whole* emotional response: he omits only expressive behaviour and actions done out of emotion, which he takes to be consequences, rather than components, of the emotion (Goldie, 2000: 13). For Goldie, then, an emotion is a complex process, which takes time to unfold, and which involves many different kinds of component.

Still, not all the emotional responses described in the previous chapter will count as emotions, on Goldie's account. He holds that an emotion is an *enduring* process: a brief emotional reaction or episode, such as Alice's bristling with anger or Bill's panicky response to Monty, is not itself an emotion, but a component of emotion (Goldie, 2000: 12–14, 68–9). For Goldie, an emotion is something more like an emotional *attitude*, or at least an extended emotional episode. Hence, he emphasizes not only the complexity of emotions at any one time, but also their tendency to evolve as time passes. Consider, for example, the way in which Dan's indignation at the decision to expand his local airport gradually broadens to encompass a range of environmental issues; or the way in which a parent's love for their child gradually changes as the vulnerable baby grows into an independent adult. This is what Goldie has in mind when he describes emotions as 'dynamic'.

What about Goldie's suggestion that an emotion has a narrative structure? The idea here is that an emotion is not a disjointed set of symptoms: it unfolds in a way that is intelligible in the light of the subject's past experiences, beliefs and character. Suppose that you discover that a friend of yours is deeply resentful about the mildly condescending attitude of one of her colleagues. Initially, perhaps, you are puzzled by the depth of her resentment. But then you remember her telling you that she has always felt over-shadowed by her highly competitive older sibling; that she has been rather unfairly overlooked in a recent promotion round; and that she is, in other contexts too, inclined to brood – and suddenly her resentment makes perfect sense. It makes sense not as something that could be rationally inferred from her beliefs and values, but in the light of her particular character and history (Goldie, 2000: 12–16, 69–72).

A Complex Alternative: Emotions as Brief Reactions

As we have seen, Goldie takes emotions to be complex processes – in particular they are enduring emotional episodes or attitudes. It is worth noting, though, that there is space for another kind of complex process theory – one that identifies emotions with brief emotional *reactions*. The psychologist Paul Ekman (1992) might be viewed as endorsing a view of this kind: an emotion, Ekman suggests, typically lasts a matter of minutes or seconds (Ekman, 1994b: 56). For Ekman, Alice's bristling with anger is a paradigm case of emotion.

There is a further significant contrast between these two accounts. While Goldie suggests that emotions have a narrative structure, Ekman argues that emotions can be understood partly in terms of their evolutionary function. According to Ekman, the structure of our emotional reactions is due in part to our culture and personal experience; but they also reflect our shared evolutionary past. Hence, for Ekman, to fully understand why an instance of anger or fear unfolds in a particular way, we need to take account of the roles that anger or fear played in in the lives of our evolutionary ancestors — the kinds of challenge that these kinds of response helped them to overcome (Ekman, 1992: 171–2; 1994a: 15–16). This is quite different from the kind of narrative explanation favoured by Goldie. Still, it is hardly surprising that Goldie and Ekman disagree about how to explain why an emotion takes the form that it does, given that they disagree about what kind of process it is.

In some respects, then, the contrast between Ekman and Goldie is just as stark as the contrast between James and Solomon. Once again, though, the dispute is not ultimately about the facts. Goldie does not deny that there are emotional reactions, or that they are structured in the way that Ekman suggests (Goldie, 2000: 104–5). Nor does Ekman deny that there are enduring emotional attitudes (Ekman, 1992: 194). The dispute is over which kind of response deserves the title 'emotion'.

Goldie on the Intentionality of Emotion

Goldie holds that emotions involve thoughts, perceptions and feelings. But he does not suggest that they involve judgements or beliefs. Here, then, we have a further contrast between Goldie and Solomon: Goldie offers a different account of emotional evaluations.

An emotional evaluation, Goldie (2000: 72–83) suggests, is a 'feeling towards' the object of the emotion. By a 'feeling towards', Goldie does not mean a *bodily* feeling, but rather a particular way of experiencing or thinking of an object or situation. To use his example, imagine that you are disgusted by a particularly slimy pudding. To describe your disgust as a feeling is to imply that it has a phenomenology: there is something it is like to experience the pudding as disgusting,

just as there is something it is like to feel overheated, or to
hear a crackling sound. There is not a great deal, Goldie
admits, that one can do to capture the experience in words.
This, though, is true of phenomenology in general: it is just
as hard to describe what it is like to feel too hot or to hear
a crackling sound. *"phenomenology"*

As well as having a distinctive phenomenology, 'feelings
towards' objects and situations represent them in certain
ways: as revolting, dangerous, glorious, and so on. In other
words, they are intentional states. Nevertheless, Goldie does
not think that these feelings are beliefs; nor does he think that
they are judgements in Solomon's sense. In many ways, he
suggests, they are more like *perceptual* experiences, though
he denies that they are *literally* perceptions. Rather, he thinks,
they constitute a distinct class of intentional state (Goldie,
2009: 237–8).

Why does Goldie deny that 'feelings towards' are beliefs?
In fact, he draws a number of contrasts between these states,
but there is one that is particularly significant. Beliefs, Goldie
argues, involve a kind of commitment to the truth that is
absent in cases of emotion. To see the point, consider the
following sentences:

'Spiders are not really dangerous, but I am scared of them.' *emo. eval.*

'Spiders are not really dangerous, but I believe that they
are.' *belief judg*

There seems to be nothing especially odd about the first sentence. It is not that hard to imagine someone experiencing an
emotion while at the same time being aware that their feelings
are not appropriate to the situation. Admittedly, in this first
case, we might say that the speaker's fear is irrational. But
this kind of irrationality is of a familiar and unsurprising
kind. In contrast, the second sentence looks distinctly odd. It
is hard to imagine how someone could consciously believe
something, while at the same time being aware that it is not
in fact the case. At the very least, one would have to assume
that the speaker is confused in a serious and puzzling way.
As Goldie points out, this seems to be an important contrast
between an emotional evaluation and a belief (Goldie, 2000:

74–6). This point does not apply only to beliefs: if we substitute the word 'judge' for the word 'believe' in the second sentence, the sentence looks just as odd, and for just the same reason. Arguably, then, Goldie has supplied a reason to doubt not only that emotional evaluations are beliefs, but also that they are judgements.

Goldie on Bodily Feelings

As we have seen, 'feelings towards' are not bodily feelings. Nevertheless, Goldie holds that bodily feelings are also an important component of emotion. Moreover, like Solomon, Goldie tries to connect the bodily phenomenology of emotion with its intentionality. However, he does this in a slightly different way.

Suppose that you have come across a particularly knotty paragraph in a philosophy book. As you struggle with the tortured prose, you become increasingly frustrated. As you frown at the page, you sense a tightness in your forehead, and you begin to feel restless and hot. These are bodily feelings. On Goldie's analysis, they are quite distinct from your frustrated 'feeling towards' the paragraph and its author. Nevertheless, as far as your *conscious experience* goes, Goldie thinks, these two kinds of feeling are impossible to separate: you experience them together, as a unity. As a result, he suggests, you may well come to experience your bodily feelings as *themselves* directed towards the object of your frustration: it seems to you *as if* your physical restlessness and tension are directed at the incomprehensible paragraph. Conversely, your frustrated 'feeling towards' the paragraph may itself come to have a bodily feel to it, as a result of its intimate association with the bodily feelings that it typically prompts. The bodily feeling, Goldie suggests, is 'thoroughly infused with the intentionality of the emotion; and in turn, the feeling towards is infused with a bodily characterization' (Goldie, 2000: 57)

Like Solomon, then, Goldie tries to link the intentionality of emotion with its bodily phenomenology. But while Solomon suggests that bodily feelings might be regarded as judgements in their own right, Goldie suggests only that bodily feelings *borrow* the intentionality of emotional evaluations. His point is, first and foremost, a point about how we *experience* these bodily feelings.

Solomon and Goldie: Contrast and Comparison

In my discussion, I have tried to bring out three key aspects of Goldie's account. First, Goldie disagrees with Solomon and James about what an emotion is: he takes it to be a complex process, involving a variety of psychological and physiological changes. As a result, Goldie does not need to decide whether an emotion is a bodily feeling or an emotional evaluation: it includes both. More precisely, Goldie takes an emotion to be an enduring and evolving process – something like an emotional attitude. In this respect, his account also contrasts with that of Ekman, who takes emotions to be brief emotional reactions.

Secondly, Goldie agrees with Solomon in foregrounding the intentionality of emotion. Nevertheless, he offers a rather different account of what an emotional evaluation is. Rather than identifying emotional evaluations with beliefs or judgements, he takes them to constitute a distinct class of intentional state – 'feelings towards' – which in many ways are more like perceptions than beliefs.

Thirdly, like Solomon, Goldie tries to forge a connection between the intentionality of emotion and its bodily phenomenology. He suggests that, in emotion, we experience 'feelings towards' and bodily feelings as a unity. As a result, we come to experience our bodily feelings as directed at objects or situations in the world.

Jesse Prinz: Back to the Body

Solomon and Goldie might both be seen as reacting against James's account of emotions as bodily feelings. In contrast, Jesse Prinz's (2004) account is very much in the spirit of James. In particular, Prinz thinks that James was right (or at least nearly right) to identify emotions with bodily feelings.

However, he accepts that James's account needs to be modified, in order to account for the intentionality of emotion.

I shall start by considering what Prinz takes an emotion to be. Earlier, I contrasted two different ways of answering this question. James and Solomon (at least in his earlier writings) take an emotion to be a particular component of an emotional response – a bodily feeling or an emotional evaluation. In contrast, Goldie and Ekman take emotions to be complex processes, which involve many different components. For reasons we will examine in Chapter 4, Prinz rejects the complex process view: he thinks that the emotion should be identified with a particular component of the emotional response. To be more precise, he thinks it should be identified with a *pair* of components, taken in combination. But which components should we pick? Should we identify emotions with emotional evaluations? Or should we take them to be bodily feelings? Prinz's point is that we do not need to choose between these two possibilities.

To understand why, it is helpful to recall Solomon's suggestion that bodily feelings might be viewed as 'judgements of the body'. Prinz's own proposal is a close cousin of Solomon's. Bodily feelings, he argues, are caused by bodily changes; their job, though, is not to alert us to those changes: rather, it is to alert us to the kind of situation we are in. The fluttering in Bill's chest, for example, might be caused by his racing heart and shallow breathing; but what it *tells* him is that he is in danger. As Prinz puts it, his bodily feelings constitute an 'embodied appraisal' of the situation (Prinz, 2004: 55–60). An 'embodied appraisal', Prinz argues, is typically accompanied by a 'valence marker' – a signal that tags the situation as good or bad (Prinz, 2004: 163). Together, these two elements go on to prompt further psychological and behavioural responses: for example, they might dispose the subject to try to escape (Prinz, 2004: 194). Together, they constitute the subject's emotional evaluation of the situation; and together, Prinz argues, they constitute the emotion. This is why, on Prinz's view, we do not need to choose between a theory of emotion that emphasizes bodily feelings and one that emphasizes emotional evaluations. Emotional evaluations just *are* bodily feelings, together with their accompanying valence markers.

As I mentioned earlier, Prinz's notion of an embodied appraisal is very similar to Solomon's notion of a 'judgement of the body'. However, Prinz and Solomon do not make quite the same use of this idea. For Solomon, as we saw earlier, an emotional evaluation is made up of a *set* of judgements, of which a 'judgement of the body' is just one. For Prinz, an emotional evaluation just *is* an embodied appraisal, along with its accompanying valence marker.

This produces an important disparity between Prinz's account and Solomon's. As we have seen, Solomon emphasizes the idea that emotions are about particular objects and events in the environment: Bill's fear, for example, is a fear *of Monty*. This is possible on Solomon's account because Bill's fearful evaluation includes not only a 'judgement of the body', but also judgements of a more conventional kind about Monty and the danger he poses. On Prinz's account, in contrast, Bill's fear is constituted *only* by his embodied appraisal. This alerts him to the danger, but it tells him nothing about the *source* of the danger. His fear, then, is about danger, but it is not about Monty. When we say that Bill is afraid of Monty, Prinz thinks, we mean only that his fear is *associated with* perceptions and thoughts about Monty (Prinz, 2004: 62). In fact, we met this kind of move before, when we considered James's account. Moreover, I suggested there that it is open to question: we do not treat other bodily feelings – for example, nausea caused by smelling a rotten egg – in the same way. We might wonder, then, whether Prinz's account faces a similar objection. I shall return to this issue in Chapter 5.

What causes the bodily changes that generate our emotions? Like James, Prinz holds that they can be caused in a variety of ways. In some cases, he thinks, the bodily changes are caused by thoughts or judgements: if someone is anxious about an examination, for example, the cause might well be the judgement that they have not spent enough time revising. In other cases, though, our emotions depend only on perceptions: the mere sight of a snake, Prinz suggests, can make the heart race. Moreover, Prinz's account is consistent with the possibility that emotions might be produced by drugs, or by electrical stimulation of the brain. Hence, on Prinz's account, our emotions will sometimes reflect our beliefs and values;

but there is no reason to assume that this is always the case (Prinz, 2004: 74–6).

Finally, it is worth noting that Prinz does not take his account to apply to all cases of emotion. In particular, he wants to allow for more enduring emotional phenomena, such as Ceri's jealousy or Dan's indignation. He calls these enduring responses 'attitudinal emotions'. As he recognizes, it would not make sense to identify attitudinal emotions with embodied appraisals, for embodied appraisals will almost certainly be relatively brief occurrences. Rather, on Prinz's account, Dan's indignation will be made up of two components: first, Dan is disposed to undergo certain bodily changes whenever he thinks about the government's decision; and, secondly, he is disposed to have certain kinds of thought about the situation – for example, the thought that the government's decision is outrageous (Prinz, 2004: 179–82). In some ways, Prinz's account of long-term attitudinal emotions is rather similar to Solomon's theory.

Summary

I have used this discussion to highlight certain questions that we might ask about emotion and to consider how some different theorists have tried to answer those questions. There are three questions I particularly want to flag up.

(1) *What is an emotion?* As we have seen, James, Solomon and Prinz distinguish between the complex emotional response and the emotion itself. The emotion itself, they think, should be identified with some particular component (or components) of the emotional response. Nevertheless, these theorists do not agree which component to pick on. James picks on bodily feelings; Solomon emphasizes emotional evaluations; while Prinz's answer covers both these things. In contrast, Goldie and Ekman argue that an emotion is a complex process, involving a range of physiological and psychological phenomena. Again, though, they disagree about what *sort* of process an emotion is: whether it is an enduring emotional attitude or a brief emotional reaction. I shall return to this question in Chapter 4.

(2) *What is an emotional evaluation?* Here, we have encountered three suggestions. According to Solomon, an emotional evaluation is a judgement, or rather a cluster of judgements (including perhaps 'judgements of the body'). Goldie, in contrast, argues that an emotional evaluation is distinctive kind of intentional state, which he calls a 'feeling towards'. Prinz, meanwhile, argues that bodily feelings themselves constitute embodied appraisals of the situation. I shall address this question in Chapter 5.

(3) *How should we explain why people's emotional responses take the form that they do?* For Solomon, the answer lies primarily with the subject's judgements. If we want to know, for example, why anger motivates people to retaliate or why gratitude motivates people to reciprocate, we need to understand how angry or grateful people take the world to be. Goldie, in contrast, argues that complex emotional responses have a narrative structure: to understand them, we need to relate them to the subject's personal history and character. Ekman suggests yet another way of understanding the shape of an emotional response: that is, by appealing to its function. We might wonder whether these different pictures are really in conflict, and if so which we should prefer. I shall investigate this question in Chapter 3.

Within these three debates, we can find some more specific questions about emotion. One question concerns our capacity to *control* our emotions. None of the theorists considered here suggest that our emotions are wholly outside our control. But they do disagree about *how* we can control our emotions and, in particular, about whether we can control them directly. Another area of controversy concerns the *phenomenology* of emotion. Do some accounts of emotional phenomenology overemphasize the role of the body in determining how it feels to be sad, or angry or afraid? And how, if at all, does the phenomenology of emotion connect with its intentionality? I shall return to all these questions in Chapter 5. Finally, Solomon stresses the idea that an emotional evaluation presents the situation as one that has a particular kind of *personal significance* for the subject. How, though, is this notion of significance to be understood? We shall meet this question again in Chapter 6.

Further Reading

All the theorists discussed in this chapter are well worth further scrutiny. For James's account, see James (1884, 1890: Chap. 25). For a contemporary defence of James's view, see Whiting (2011). To trace Solomon's developing views, see Solomon (1993 [1976]: esp. Chap. 5, 2003a [1988], 2003b, 2003c, 2007). The other accounts discussed here can be found in Ekman (1992) and Prinz (2004: esp. Chaps 1–3). Other important general accounts of emotion published in recent years include Griffiths (1997: esp. Part 1); Ben Ze'ev (2000: Part 1); Nussbaum (2001: Chaps 1 and 2); Roberts (2003: esp. Chap. 2); Robinson (2005: Part 1); Deonna and Teroni (2012).

2
Emotion, Coherence and Function

Introduction

A Plan of Attack

I ended the previous chapter by highlighting three questions about emotion:

- What is an emotion?
- What is an emotional evaluation?
- How should we explain why people's emotional responses take the form that they do?

We might expect a discussion of emotion to begin by addressing the first of these questions. Here, however, I shall start with the third. In particular, I want to investigate the following claim:

> One important way in which we can explain why emotional responses take the form that they do is by appealing to their functional properties.

In what follows, I shall refer to this as the *functional claim*. In this chapter, I shall explain what I take this claim to imply and I shall offer some considerations in its defence. As a result, I shall postpone my discussion of what an emotion is until Chapter 4; and I shall not address the nature of emotional evaluations until Chapter 5. Still, I do have a reason for adopting this apparently eccentric plan: some of my arguments in Chapter 4 rely on the functional claim. This is why I need to begin by explaining what it is and why I think that it is plausible.

Nevertheless, in reading this chapter, it is important to remember that I am not talking about emotions as such. This is because I have not yet said what, if anything, I take an emotion to be. The functional claim is a claim about how we should explain the structure of a complex emotional *response* – an emotional reaction, episode or attitude.

Structural Questions

Why does an angry response characteristically involve a desire to retaliate? Why do people blush when they are embarrassed? Why does grief come to an end? These are all questions about the form or structure of an emotional response. In what follows, I shall refer to them as *structural questions*. In this chapter, I want to consider how we might go about answering questions of this kind. I shall start by saying a little more about structural questions themselves. In particular, I want to distinguish them from another type of question that might seem rather similar. I shall also explain why we should not assume that all structural questions can be answered in the same way.

Suppose that Ella comes home from work, clutching a bunch of daffodils, which she tenderly proffers to Fred. 'Why did you buy those?' he asks. 'Out of love!' she replies. Fred's question concerns Ella's action: he is asking why she acted as she did. Her reply makes sense of her action by pointing to the motivation that lay behind it – a loving desire for Fred's happiness. Similarly, suppose that Fred confesses to Ella that, as a child, he once set fire to his sister's homework. 'Why?' Ella asks in surprise. 'Out of envy,' he replies, ruefully. Once again, Fred's explanation makes sense of his action by revealing the kind of motivation that prompted it – an envious desire to hurt his sister. Later, Fred finds himself mulling over these exchanges. 'I understand that Ella acted out of a loving concern for my happiness; and I understand that I acted out of an envious desire to hurt my sister. But there is still something that puzzles me. Why does Ella's love for me imply that she cares about my happiness? Why did envying my sister mean that I wanted to hurt her? Why should love and envy *be like that*?'

The point of this story is to draw out a distinction between two kinds of question. On the one hand, we can ask why someone *acted* as they did – a question that might sometimes be answered by citing their emotional response. On the other hand, we can take a step back and ask about the emotional response *itself*: why does that type of emotional response involve wanting to act in that way? This is what I mean by a structural question.

Structural questions need not be about emotional desires and actions. We can also ask why a certain type of emotional response characteristically involves certain kinds of thought or feeling. We can ask, too, about its duration, or about the kinds of situation that prompt it. We might wonder, for example, why it seems strange to say that someone was in love for just five minutes; or why we tend to love fewer people than we like.

We can also distinguish between two kinds of structural question. My examples so far have been what I shall call 'broad-brush' structural questions: they are questions about love *in general*, or envy *in general*. But we can also ask structural questions about the details of a particular case of love or envy – for example, Ella's love for Fred, or Fred's envious attitude towards his sister. Why, Fred might wonder, did Ella choose to express her love with *daffodils*? (Why not roses?) Why did his envy fade when his baby brother was born? I shall call these 'fine-grained' structural questions. In this chapter, I am especially interested in questions of the broad-brush kind.

How should we go about answering structural questions? It is unlikely that this question has a simple answer. As we have seen, emotional responses have many different components and features, and there is no reason to assume that these can all be explained in the same way. We cannot assume, either, that broad-brush and fine-grained questions invite similar kinds of answer. Hence, my aim in this chapter is not to champion a single approach. Rather, I want just to *make room* for a particular approach – one that appeals to functional considerations.

Explaining Structure: Three Approaches

There is, of course, no guarantee that structural questions have interesting answers. If I ask why love characteristically involves wanting one's beloved to be happy, the answer might be that there is no explanation at all: it is just a matter of chance. More plausibly, the explanation might be merely anatomical: perhaps there is something about the structure of the brain that ensures that loving evaluations are associated with certain kinds of desire. These boring suggestions cannot be ruled out. Still, there is a good reason to think that structural questions often have interesting answers. As I mentioned in Chapter 1, emotional responses are characteristically *coherent* responses – responses that make sense as ways of dealing with a particular kind of situation. These two boring suggestions leave the coherence of emotional responses unexplained.

In what follows, I shall assume that structural questions often do have interesting answers. I shall consider three different kinds of answer that might be proposed.

(1) *Intentional answers.* We might try to answer structural questions by appealing to the intentional content of the subject's emotional evaluation – how the subject takes the situation to be. This suggestion looks particularly plausible when we focus on emotional desires and actions. For example, it makes sense that Fred should want to hurt his sister, given that he takes her to be a rival for his parents' affection. How this suggestion should be developed will depend on what we take an emotional evaluation to be. As we saw in Chapter 2, Solomon holds that emotional evaluations are judgements (Solomon, 1993 [1976], 2003a [1988]). On this view, emotional evaluations present *reasons* for the subject's desires and actions: Fred, perhaps, takes his rivalry with his sister as a reason to try to hurt her. Prinz (2004), in contrast, denies that emotional evaluations are judgements. On his account, Fred's emotional evaluation *impels* him to try to change the

situation, much as physical pain might impel someone to escape the source of their pain. In either case, though, it might be suggested that it is the content of Fred's emotional evaluation – the way in which he represents the situation – that explains his action.

(2) *Narrative answers*. In Chapter 2, we also met Goldie's suggestion that emotional responses have a narrative structure. To explain how an emotional response develops, Goldie suggests, we need to consider how it fits into the subject's life as a whole – how it relates to their character and past history. Given that this approach emphasizes the experiences and traits of particular individuals, it looks particularly suited to answering fine-grained structural questions. Suppose, for example, that we want to understand why Fred chose to burn his sister's homework, rather than her diary. We may not get very far, Goldie thinks, by examining Fred's beliefs about the situation: it might turn out that it is very hard to make any rational sense of his behaviour. We might do better by considering what sort of person he is and what his experiences have been (Goldie, 2000: 12–16, 69–72).

(3) *Functional answers*. Finally, in Chapter 2 we also met the suggestion that the structure of an emotional response might be explained in *functional* terms. Theorists of emotion have long suggested that our emotions function to help us satisfy basic needs. In the eighteenth century, the philosopher Francis Hutcheson made the point in particularly striking terms: the passions, he suggested, 'form a machine, most accurately subservient to the necessities, convenience and happiness of a rational system' (Hutcheson 2002 [1728]: 120). More recently, evolutionary psychologists have argued that our emotional capacities evolved as responses to 'fundamental life tasks' faced by our evolutionary ancestors (Ekman, 1992).[1] Social constructivists, in contrast, argue that emotions are cultural phenomena, which perform important social functions (Averill, 1980; Armon-Jones, 1986).

These suggestions point to another way of explaining why an emotional response takes the form that it does: by appealing to its functional properties. Suppose that someone is wondering why anger has certain characteristic features. Why, they might ask, is anger characteristically elicited in certain situations, but not in others? Why are angry people motivated to attack or threaten the person who is the target of their anger? Why does anger often fade as soon as the other person backs down? All this makes sense if we suppose that the function of an angry response is to fend off an aggressive challenge from another person.

In this section, I have identified three sets of considerations to which we might appeal in answering structural questions – intentional, narrative and functional. These three suggestions all seem well worth considering. Indeed, it seems plausible that they all have a role to play. In what follows, though, I want to focus on just one of these approaches – the functional approach. As I mentioned earlier, this is because I need to appeal to the functional claim later on. In the following section, I shall explain what I take a function to be; in the final section, I shall discuss, and try to defend, the functional claim.

What Is a Function?

A Historical Theory of Functions

Many of the things that people make are designed to perform one or more specific functions: the function of a paperclip is to fasten pieces of paper together; one function of CERN's Large Hadron Collider is to cause protons to collide. Biological phenomena – biological organs, systems, traits and behaviours – are also said to have functions: the function of a porcupine's spines is to protect it from predators; one function of the liver is to store vitamin A.

Things that have functions are supposed to perform them, but there is no guarantee that they will. A porcupine's spines might fail to protect it because they are malformed, or because the porcupine dies before it ever meets a predator. Equally, something might be used to perform a task that is not its function: for example, a walker might use a discarded porcupine spine as an impromptu hat pin. A function, then, is not simply what something does; it is not even something useful that it does. How, then, can we distinguish something's function from other things that it happens to do?

Larry Wright (1976) suggested that to ascribe a function to something is to make a claim about its *history*. Consider the spines of a particular porcupine, Portia. Portia's spines function to protect her from predators. To say that they have this function, on Wright's account, is to imply the following:

W1 Portia's spines exist, in part, *because* porcupines' spines sometimes protect them from predators.

In this case, the truth of W1 presupposes something like the following story: Portia's ancestors had spines, which sometimes protected them from predators; by doing this, they helped Portia's ancestors to survive and to reproduce successfully; as result, Portia was born and developed spines of her own. Again, consider the paperclip on my desk. Its function, I suggested, is to fasten pieces of paper together. According to Wright, this implies the following:

W2 This paperclip exists, in part, *because* paperclips sometimes fasten pieces of paper together.

The story behind W2 is likely to be rather different from Portia's: it will refer to the way in which people have used paperclips in the past, or perhaps the intentions of paperclip manufacturers. On Wright's account, though, the details of these stories do not matter. What matters is just that there is some kind of explanatory connection between (a) the fact that an object exists and (b) the fact that similar objects do a particular job.

I think that Wright's approach to functions is a good one.[2] In particular, it can help us make sense of the idea that something's function is something that it is *supposed* to do and not something that it just happens to do. As it stands, however, the account overlooks two important points.

First, something's function is not just something that it is supposed to do, but something that it is supposed to contribute to something *else*.[3] By performing its function, an object helps some other mechanism, system or agent to achieve a particular outcome.

To see why this matters, think about the following claim:

W3   I exist, in part, because people breathe.

W3 seems to be true: if my ancestors had never drawn breath, I would not exist today. Still, it seems rather odd to say that it is my *function* to breathe, in the way that the function of a paperclip is to fasten pieces of paper together. It seems odd, I would suggest, because the story behind W3 differs from the stories behind W1 and W2. By fastening pieces of paper together, paperclips have helped people to keep their papers tidy. By deterring predators, porcupines' spines have helped porcupines to survive. But by breathing, my ancestors helped *themselves* to survive. This is why breathing is not a function of mine: it is not something that I am supposed to contribute to some larger system or to some other agent. Wright's account needs to be adjusted to take account of this point.

Secondly, something's function must be something it does *by itself*, not something that it does in concert with other things (Neander, 1995: 118–20; Price, 2001: 61–2). This matters because we often appeal to the functions of artefacts and biological organs to classify them into types: what makes something a liver, rather than a spleen or a pancreas, is in part a matter of the functions that it has. This will be possible, though, only if the liver's functions are distinct from the functions of the spleen and the pancreas. Hence, it is no use saying that the function of the liver is to help the organism to survive, because that is true of the pancreas and spleen as well. We need to identify the *specific* ways in which the liver helps the organism to survive.

How might this work in a particular case? Consider Reynard, a fox. Like other foxes, Reynard has a thick coat of fur. Among other things, Reynard's fur helps to keep him warm. More precisely, its function is to slow the rate at which heat is lost from his body. It has this function, I am suggesting, for roughly the following reasons:

F1   Reynard's ancestors had fur that sometimes slowed the rate at which heat was lost from their bodies.

F2   Slowing heat loss was something that foxes' fur did *by itself*, and not in concert with other organs and systems of the body.

F3   By slowing heat loss, foxes' fur helped other organs or systems to produce some further outcome (e.g. keeping the fox alive).

F4   All this helps to explain why Reynard's fur exists today.

F1 and F4 embody the historical claim that is at the heart of Wright's account. F3 adds the idea that the function of a biological organ or trait is the contribution it makes to the workings of *other* biological organs or systems; while F2 makes it clear that the function of a biological organ or trait is the *specific* contribution that it makes to these other organs or systems.

There is, though, a second way in which we might describe this contribution: foxes' fur traps warm air close to their skins. Indeed, it is just *by* doing this that it slows the loss of heat from their bodies. Why not say, then, that the function of Reynard's fur is to trap warm air close to his skin? This is, I admit, a rather pernickety point: I am raising it here only because it will be important in a later chapter. It is also open to debate. My own view is that trapping warm air is *not* a function of Reynard's fur: rather, it is *the way in which* it performs its function.[4] The function of foxes' fur is what it *directly* contributes to their other organs and systems – that is, slowing the loss of heat. To accommodate this point we need to make a slight adjustment to F3:

F3*   By slowing heat loss, foxes' fur *directly* helped other organs or systems to produce some further outcome (e.g. keeping the fox alive).

To sum up, then: the function of Reynard's fur is the *specific* and *direct* contribution that his ancestors' fur made to other organs and systems in their bodies, so helping to ensure that Reynard (and his fur) exists today.

Normal Performance

Before moving on, there is one further functional notion that I need to introduce. I have suggested that a fox's fur performs its function in a particular way – by trapping warm air. To be more precise, this is how foxes' fur has *historically* performed its function. Conceivably, though, a fox's fur might occasionally perform its function in some novel or unusual way. Suppose that Reynard is adopted by sentimental humans, charmed by his thick fur: Reynard's fur now slows heat loss, not only by trapping warm air close to his skin, but also by giving him access to a warm house. In doing this, it is fulfilling its function, but not in the way in which foxes' fur has done so in the past. To borrow some terminology from Ruth Millikan (1984: 33–4), it is not performing its function in a *normal* way. Whenever I use the word 'normal' in this book, I will always use it in this functional, historical sense, and never just to mean 'typically' or 'most of the time'.

Some Implications

I shall end this section by highlighting four implications of this account of functions.

(1) *Varieties of history.* In setting out this account, I have focused particularly on biological examples – cases in which something's function rests on its evolutionary history. There are, though, other possibilities. The function of a social custom will depend on its *cultural* history. In certain cultures, for example, bowing functions as a way to signal respect: this form of behaviour persists in those cultures just because bowing is an effective way to show respect (Millikan, 1984: 24). In other cases, the function of a trait or habit depends on the *personal* history of its owner. For example, I sometimes tie my shoe laces together at night when I need to remember something in the morning. For me, tying my laces together has come to function as a reminder.

(2) *The modesty of function ascriptions.* On the historical account, to say that the function of Reynard's fur is to slow heat loss is to make a very modest claim: it implies that, in the past, foxes' fur *sometimes* slowed heat loss, and that this *sometimes* helped foxes to survive. It does not imply that foxes' fur does this infallibly or even reliably, or that having fur is the most effective way of slowing heat loss that the foxes might have developed. It is not even to say that foxes'

fur successfully performs this function today: changes in the environment might mean that foxes' fur can no longer perform this function.

(3) *Function and evidence.* This historical approach implies that function ascriptions are often partly speculative. When I make claims about the function of Reynard's fur, I cannot prove my point by appealing to what his fur actually does now or what it is good at doing: what it does now may not be what it evolved to do. At best, considerations of this kind provide *some reason* to think that Reynard's fur has a particular function: they are inferences to the best explanation.

(2) *Function and explanation.* On the historical account, the notion of a function is always an *explanatory* notion: we can appeal to something's function to explain why it exists; and we can often appeal to something's function, and how it normally performs its function, to explain why it takes the form that it does. That porcupines' quills are sharp, for example, *makes sense*, given that their function is to protect the porcupine from predators, and given that they normally do this by jabbing would-be attackers.

Emotion and Function

The Functional Claim Again

Earlier, I mentioned the functional claim:

> One important way in which we can explain why emotional responses take the form that they do is by appealing to their functional properties.

In this section, I shall explain how I am going to understand this claim, drawing on the account of functions set out in the previous section. Having done that, I shall try to defend it.

The functional claim implies, first, that any given type of emotional response follows a fixed pattern: it is a matter of instinct or habit. We do not need to assume that every detail of the response can be viewed in this way: that would be very implausible. What matters is that there is *some* recognizable pattern – a pattern of evaluation, feeling and motivation, say – discernible at some very broad level of description. It implies, too, that this pattern has a certain kind of history. As we have seen, though, there is room for disagreement about the details of the story. It may be that our emotional capacities have been shaped by natural selection to perform specific biological functions. Alternatively, our emotional responses may be the products of our cultural history, or of the personal histories of individual subjects.

In fact, we do not need to choose between these possibilities: emotional responses may well have functions of *all* these kinds. Consider, for example, the case of anger. We might speculate that our capacity for anger is inherited from our evolutionary ancestors: it evolved, perhaps, to counter aggressive or disrespectful behaviour by other agents. It is plausible, though, that the particular *ways* in which people experience and display anger are strongly influenced both by cultural norms and by personal experience. In one society, for example, displays of anger might play a role in enforcing social norms; while in another, they might function as a call for help. For one individual, displays of anger might be a means of drawing attention to themselves; while for someone else, they might function as a way of deflecting criticism. Moreover, these cultural and personal considerations might have a significant role to play in determining how a particular angry response develops – for example, the kinds of thoughts and motivations it involves.

These various possibilities threaten to make discussion of this issue unmanageably complicated. For the purposes of this book, I am going to help myself to a specific set of empirical assumptions. I shall assume, first, that the psychological and physiological mechanisms that produce our emotional responses have an evolutionary origin. Hence, when I talk about the functions of these mechanisms, I shall treat them as *biological* mechanisms, shaped by natural selection. At the same time, I shall assume that the way in which these mechanisms normally operate in any particular individual is strongly influenced by culture and by personal experience. Cultural and personal factors, I shall assume, help to determine the kinds of situation that elicit an emotional response, the ways in which people experience and display emotion, and the role that different kinds of emotional response play in their personal lives.

As I mentioned earlier, the historical theory of functions implies that function ascriptions have very modest implications. To say that emotional responses have functions is not to imply that they are always an effective response to the situation. It is not even to imply that emotional responses are *ever* effective in a modern environment: conceivably, emotions such as rage or sexual jealousy no longer have a useful role to play. In what follows, I shall assume that emotional responses do sometimes fulfil their functions. But this does not simply follow from the claim that they have them. We should remember, too, that specific claims about the functions of emotional responses will inevitably have a speculative character: they are based on an inference to the best explanation.[5]

Finally, on the historical account, the notion of a function is always an *explanatory* one. Hence, if emotional responses have functions, we should be able to appeal to their functional properties to explain why they take the form that they do. In particular, we might expect that functional considerations will be particularly helpful in answering *broad-brush* structural questions – questions about the structure of anger in general, or love in general. In contrast, the fine-grained features of an emotional response are likely to be influenced by the details of the situation, by the subject's character and by their beliefs and values. Moreover, the more extended the emotional response, the more scope there will be for these other influences to play a role: an emotional reaction may well be relatively predictable; but an emotional attitude can develop in all sorts of ways, depending on the circumstances, the subject's beliefs, and so on.

Nevertheless, there is a proviso to be made: I have allowed that a certain type of emotional response – anger, say – might come to have a specific function for a particular individual. In this kind of case, some of the fine-grained features of an angry response might well be explained by these functional considerations. Indeed, in a case of this kind, the functional explanation might also be a narrative one, in that it seeks to explain the subject's response by placing it in the context of their personal history.

Why, though, should we believe the functional claim? I shall end by explaining why I think that the claim is plausible, and by addressing a couple of specific objections that might be raised to it.

Why Believe the Functional Claim?

As I mentioned earlier, the idea that emotional responses can be understood in functional terms has a long history. It is not obvious, though, that the claim is correct. Emotional responses may not have functional properties at all. Moreover, even if they do, it does not follow that we need to appeal to their functional properties to answer structural questions: perhaps intentional and narrative explanations can do all the work. These are primarily empirical questions, which depend on the history of the mechanisms that generate emotional responses and on the ways in which those mechanisms work. Hence they are not issues that can be settled definitively here. But I do want to explain why I find the functional claim attractive.

Someone who wants to defend the functional claim might begin by pointing to the apparent *coherence* of emotional responses. Suppose, for example, that Gregor has lost his temper with his neighbour Hayley, who has just said something disparaging about his personal habits: he is seething, and has a strong urge to yell at her. His anger certainly looks like a response that has been designed to deal with offence. This is hardly decisive, however. Even if the coherence claim is true, there are other ways in which it might be explained. In particular, we might try to explain it in intentional terms.

To see this, compare the following case. This morning, I noticed that the light bulb in my bathroom needed changing. This produced various effects: I girded myself for action; I searched the kitchen cupboard for a new bulb; and so on. This, I take it, was a perfectly coherent response to the situation. But that does not imply that I am in possession of a 'light bulb changing response' which functions to help me to deal with extinct light bulbs. I acted as I did because I *saw* that the bulb needed changing and because I *believed* that I would find a new bulb in the cupboard. Similarly, it might be suggested that Gregor's urge to shout at Hayley makes sense, given that he takes her remarks to be offensive and believes that shouting at her would be an appropriate way to deter further comment.

This intentional solution, though, faces an objection: emotional desires and behaviour sometimes seem to run counter to the subject's beliefs. Suppose, for example, that Gregor realizes that it would be quite *counterproductive* to yell at Hayley: the most effective response, he believes, would be to deliver a cool stare. Even so, it seems quite possible that, in his anger, he still has a strong urge to yell. Indeed, this kind of situation seems common enough: someone suddenly confronted by a mountain lion might turn and flee, even though they know that they would be safer staying still; a parent, taking their child to school for the first time, might be desperate to shower them with kisses at the school gate, even though they know this will make the parting more difficult.

Seen from an intentional perspective, these kinds of situation seem *puzzling*: why should people be motivated to behave in ways that they believe will make the situation worse? These are not cases in which the subject is torn between two conflicting goals – eating cheesecake and being healthy, say. Gregor's desire to behave coolly and his urge to yell are directed at exactly the *same* goal – putting Hayley in her place. Why should he feel an urge to take a means to his goal that he believes to be ineffective?

It might be suggested that we can solve this problem by recalling Solomon's account. According to Solomon, Gregor's anger is not simply the judgement that Hayley's comments are offensive: it involves a *complex* of judgements – including, perhaps, the judgement that this is the kind of situation that calls for an aggressive response. Hence, to describe Gregor as angry implies that he *does* believe that he should yell at Hayley, even if – at the same time – he has also made the conflicting judgement that it would be best to behave coolly. Later, in Chapter 5, I am going to argue that conflicts between emotion and judgement are not plausibly viewed as conflicts between two judgements. Here, though, I shall just note that this solution seems to raise more questions than it answers. Why is Gregor so ready to judge that he should yell at Hayley, given that his evidence points in the other direction? Once he recognizes that shouting at Hayley would be counterproductive, why does he not just change his mind? This suggestion allows us to explain Gregor's urge in terms of his beliefs, but it does so only at the cost of making his *beliefs* seem very puzzling.

Could we explain the situation in narrative terms? It is not clear that this will help – at least, not in every case. As we have seen, narrative considerations seem to be most useful when we are explaining the fine-grained features of an emotional response. On the face of it, though, the urge to yell at the offender is a decidedly broad-brush feature of anger. Moreover, in some cases of this kind, the subject's behaviour is puzzling, not only from an intentional perspective, but from a narrative perspective too: yelling at someone might be thoroughly out of character for Gregor.

Even so, Gregor's urge to yell does not seem to be a mere aberration. Anger does, after all, commonly involve a desire to behave aggressively. Moreover, viewed from a functional perspective, this makes sense: behaving aggressively can be an effective way to cause an opponent to back down. Here, then, we do have a way to make sense of Gregor's urge. For this explanation to work, we need to assume that his urge is a fixed feature of his angry reaction – an inherited trait or a learned habit. Moreover, we need to assume that it is there just because aggressive behaviour has, in the past, sometimes proved to be an effective way to deal with offence. If this were so, it would hardly be surprising that Gregor is motivated to behave in this way: that is how angry people *normally* want to behave.

I am suggesting, then, that appealing to functional considerations can enable us to explain an otherwise puzzling feature of some emotional responses. It allows us to explain why emotional responses sometimes involve desires that are at odds with the subject's beliefs and values. In particular, it allows to explain why these desires, misplaced though they may be, do not seem to be mere aberrations. This is, I take it, a point in favour of the functional claim. It constitutes a reason to think both that emotional responses do have functions, and that functional explanations are not always crowded out by explanations of other kinds. This is not to deny that intentional and narrative considerations also have important roles to play: I am claiming only that functional considerations are a significant part of the story.

Even with all these provisos, however, this suggestion may well prompt some concerns. I shall end by briefly considering two possible objections to it.

Too Crass for Comfort?

One objection is that functional explanations are crassly reductive. Suppose, for example, that I were to apply this functional approach to love. I might speculate, perhaps, that the function of love is to enable people to develop intimate and lasting personal relationships with others. It does this, in part, by motivating the subject to spend time with their beloved, to protect them and to try to win their love in return. Once we realize this, I might argue, we can begin to answer some of the questions I have raised about love in the course of this discussion: why we tend to care about the happiness of the people we love; why it seems odd to say that one was in love for just five minutes; why we are inclined to love such a small number of people.[6] However, to describe love in these terms, the objection goes, is to miss its personal and ethical importance. It is to present love as a mere drive, imposed on us by our biology or culture, and divorced from our personal concerns. To understand love, we need to approach it from a personal perspective: we need to describe how love feels to the people involved; how love shapes, and is shaped by, their beliefs and goals; how it helps to give value or meaning to their lives. To do this, we need to focus on people's beliefs and desires; or perhaps, as Goldie suggests, their character and personal history.

I have some sympathy with this worry: as I have stressed, I do not think that functional explanations can tell us all we want to know about love or any other emotion. On the other hand, I am not convinced that functional considerations have no role to play in elucidating the personal and the ethical aspects of emotion. If my speculative story about the function of love were true, it would indeed have some bearing on what it is like to experience love, how love is likely to mesh with our concerns and values, and what role it might play in a good human life. To describe love in functional terms is not to write it off as a mere biological drive or cultural convention. Rather, it is to view it in a particular *context* – one that relates it to our needs and capacities as biological and social beings of a certain kind. This may not be all there is to say about love, but it is not to denigrate or dismiss it.

Retrospective Emotions

In illustrating my account with the case of anger and love, I selected examples that are particularly easy to explain in functional terms. It is rather less obvious, though, that we can understand other emotions in the same way. In particular, it might be argued, the functional approach cannot be applied to *retrospective* emotions – emotions concerned with past events. These include grief, regret, triumph and some cases of sorrow and joy. In these cases, it might be thought, it is hard to see what *use* our emotional response could have, since it is now too late to affect the situation. After all, there is no use in crying over spilt milk.

In response, I want to insist that there *is* some use in crying over spilt milk – for two reasons. First, when we consider the motivational component of an emotional response, we do not have to assume that its function is to motivate the subject to act there and then. The motivational effects of an emotional response might well make themselves felt only in the long term, and perhaps in quite subtle ways. Consider, for example, the case of grief. Grief often seems to influence people's long-term motivations: it can make them less willing to form new relationships or, more positively, it can spur them to make more of the relationships they have. Secondly, retrospective emotions often prompt the subject to reflect on what has happened: in sorrow and regret, for example, people characteristically ruminate on what has gone wrong; in triumph, they revel in the glorious details of their success. Moreover, emotional rumination arguably has a purpose: by reflecting on what has happened, people can come to understand better what they should be motivated to avoid or repeat in the future. Hence, even if retrospective emotions are elicited by events in the past, they may yet have a function that is directed to the future.[7] If so, there is no need to deny that retrospective emotions can sometimes be understood in functional terms.

Summary

In this chapter, I have suggested that one way in which we can explain the form of an emotional response is by appealing to its functional properties. Doing this, as we have seen, involves appealing to the ways in which emotional responses have, in the past, helped to satisfy our needs – whether as biological organisms or as individuals. This functional approach will not answer every interesting question that can be asked about emotional responses. Nevertheless, it is an approach that can be applied to many different types of response, including retrospective emotions. My aim here has been to make room for this kind of explanation. In the chapters that follow, I shall find a number of ways to put it to use.

Further Reading

For Goldie's account of the narrative structure of emotion, see Goldie (2000). His discussion is threaded through the book, so it is best to use the index. For discussions of emotion that emphasize its biological function, see Tooby and Cosmides (1990); Ekman (1992); Griffiths (1997: esp. Chap. 3). For some social constructivist approaches, see Averill (1980) and Armon-Jones (1986); see also Griffiths (1997: Chap. 6). For some more recent discussion of this debate, see Goldie (2000: Chap. 4); DeLancey (2002: Chap. 4); Prinz (2004: Chaps 5–6). For an overview of philosophical theories of function, see the entry on 'Teleological notions in biology' in the *Stanford Encyclopedia of Philosophy* (Allen, 2009). For some different versions of the historical theory of functions, see Millikan (1989); Neander (1991); Godfrey-Smith (1994); Price (2001: Part 1).

3
What Is an Emotion?

Introduction: What Is the Question?

In this chapter, I shall investigate a key question for any theorist of emotion: what exactly *is* an emotion?

The first thing to note is that the question is *ambiguous*. In fact, there are at least three different ways in which it might be understood:

Q1 What makes it right to classify a certain type of response (contempt, say) as an *emotional* response and not, say, as a mood or a bodily sensation?

Q2 How should we distinguish between different *types* of emotional response? What is the difference, for example, between contempt and anger?

Q3 What constitutes a particular *occurrence* or *instance* of emotion, such as Alice's anger at Zack when he lets the library door slam? Is her anger identical with her angry reaction as a whole? Or is it a particular *component* of her response – her angry evaluation, say, or the tense feelings that result?

It might be thought that this ambiguity does not matter very much, because these questions need to be answered together.

Consider, in particular, the relationship between Q2 and Q3. If instances of emotion are feelings, the thought goes, they must be classified by the way that they feel; if they are evaluations, they must classified by their content – by what they are about. Indeed, many theorists of emotion have answered Q2 and Q3 together: William James (1890), for example, combines the view that instances of emotion are bodily feelings with the view that they should be classified by the way they feel. However, there is no need to assume that answers to Q2 and Q3 *must* line up in this way. Jerome Shaffer (1983), for example, follows James in identifying instances of emotion with bodily feelings. But his answer to Q2 differs from James's: what distinguishes one type of emotion from another, he thinks, is partly a matter of the beliefs and desires that cause them (see also Sabini and Silver, 2005). Q2 and Q3, then, are separate questions, and I shall discuss them separately here.

As we shall see, I am not going to answer these questions in a completely straightforward way. In the case of Q1 and Q2, this is because – like many other theorists – I accept that categories such as 'emotion', 'anger', 'contempt' and 'love' are not sharply defined. There is no clear line dividing emotional responses from other kinds of psychological occurrence; nor is it always a straightforward matter to decide whether a particular response should count (say) as a case of contempt or anger. Still, I shall suggest, this does not preclude us from identifying the kinds of consideration that bear on these questions and investigating the connections between them. In the case of Q3, my approach will be rather more radical: I want to raise the possibility that we may not be able to find a satisfactory answer to this question. However, I shall also suggest that we should not be too worried by this: as theorists of emotion, we do not need an answer to Q3. My discussion of Q3 will take up the bulk of the chapter: I shall return to Q1 and Q2 in the final section.

Q3: Some Preliminaries

What would count as a *good* answer to Q3? First, I shall assume that we are looking for an answer that rests on some reasonable principle: we are not just trying to stipulate an answer. Secondly, I shall assume that we are looking for single, decisive answer to the question. Finally, I shall assume that we are looking for an answer of a kind that will be useful to us in building a philosophical theory of emotion. A good answer to Q3, then, will be one that is reasonable, decisive and theoretically useful.

How might we look for such an answer? One way to do this would be to examine all the different answers that have been suggested, in order to decide which is the most plausible. Here, I shall take a different approach: I want to look at some of the *strategies* that have been used to support particular answers. I shall argue that none of these strategies is likely to yield a good answer to Q3. Given this, I want to suggest, it is worth taking seriously the possibility that we will not be able to find such an answer.

One reason someone might have for taking this line is that they are *in general* sceptical about answering questions of this kind: they think that questions of the form 'What is an emotion?', 'What is knowledge?', 'What is art?', and so on, never have good answers. This is not the line I want to take here. Rather, I shall suggest that the problem lies with the *particular nature* of emotional responses – their diversity, their complexity and their functional coherence. More precisely, I am going to argue that *if* emotional responses have these features, it may well be impossible to find a good answer to Q3.

This conclusion is both provisional and tentative. It is provisional, because it depends on the account of emotion that I offered in Chapters 1 and 3: that account may turn out to be mistaken. It is tentative, because it is always possible that there is some other, more successful strategy for answering Q3 that I have overlooked.[1] My aim is not to drive my conclusion home. I am trying to raise a possibility, and to suggest an alternative approach.

Processes or Components?

In Chapter 2, I distinguished between two kinds of answer to Q3. On the one hand, Ekman and Goldie take instances of emotion to be complex processes, which unfold over time. As we saw there, Ekman (1992) identifies instances of emotion with emotional reactions, or perhaps very brief episodes of emotion; while, for Goldie (2000), an instance of emotion is something more like an emotional attitude. However, Ekman and Goldie agree in holding that an instance of emotion is a process, which involves a variety of components and which takes time to unfold (see also Robinson, 2005).

On the other hand, theorists such as James, Solomon and Prinz identify instances of emotion with particular components of an emotional response. According to James (1890), an emotion is a bodily feeling, while Solomon (1993 [1976]) has suggested that an emotion is an emotional evaluation.[2] Prinz (2004), meanwhile, attempts to reconcile these two suggestions: on his view, an instance of emotion is an emotional evaluation; but an emotional evaluation is, in part, a bodily feeling. Still, these theorists might all be viewed as agreeing on one thing: an instance of emotion can be identified with some particular component of an emotional response, while other components are its accompaniments, causes or effects.

It might look, then, as if we can divide these views into two groups: complex process theories and single component theories.[3] In fact, this is a simplification. For one thing, theorists who identify emotions with emotional evaluations do not always think of emotional evaluations as unitary things. Solomon (2003a [1988]), for example, holds that an emotional evaluation consists of a *system* of judgements; while Prinz takes an emotional evaluation to be made up of two distinct signals: an embodied appraisal and a valence marker. Secondly, there is room for intermediate views. In his later writings, as we have seen, Solomon has suggested that an emotion might be a combination of *two* things: judgement and feeling (Solomon, 2003a [1988]: 94–5; 2003b: 189).[4] On the other side, Goldie does not think that an instance of emotion includes *everything* that might be viewed as part of an emotional attitude: on his view, expressive behaviour and emotional actions are effects, not components, of the emotion (Goldie, 2000: 13). In reality, then, there is a spectrum of views here, rather than a neat divide.

Still, even if the division is a simplification, it does have a use: it highlights some different questions we might ask these theorists. Consider, first, theorists who emphasize particular components of the emotional response. It is not hard to see what questions we might put to them. Given the complexity of emotional responses, why pick out some particular component (or components) as having a special importance? And why pick on one component rather than another? I shall consider these questions in the following section. Again, it is not hard to see what we might ask theorists who take emotions to be complex processes. Given the diversity of emotional responses, why focus on one kind of process rather than another? I shall turn to this question in the third section.

Why does it *matter* which view we adopt? After all, none of these theorists need deny that other emotional phenomena exist or that they play an important role in our emotional lives. It matters, I would suggest, because different answers tend to direct our attention to different aspects of our emotional lives. Theories like those of Ekman and James highlight aspects of emotional experience that are transient and involuntary; they might be taken to suggest a view of emotions as short-lived upheavals, which interrupt, or even disrupt, the ordinary course of our lives. In contrast, theories like those of Goldie or Solomon highlight the meaning that our emotional responses have for us and the ways in which they connect with our beliefs and values. Of course, none of these theorists are forced to ignore other aspects of our emotional lives. But it is natural to assume that any answer we give to Q3 will both reflect and help to determine what we take to be interesting and important about emotion.

I shall begin with theorists who focus on a particular component (or set of components). The challenge for these theorists, as we have seen, is to explain why we should identify the emotion with *that* component, and not some other component, or even the response as a whole. I shall explore three different ways of meeting this challenge: the *matching strategy*, the *essentialist strategy* and the *explanatory strategy*. In each case, I shall consider how the strategy has been put to use by a particular theorist: Robert C. Roberts, William James and Jesse Prinz.

Which Component?

Robert C. Roberts: The Matching Strategy

The matching strategy involves two steps:

- describe what instances of emotion are *like*;
- look for something that uniquely *matches* this description.

Employing the matching strategy is rather like trying to catch a murderer by asking witnesses to agree on a description of the killer and then looking for someone who matches that description. On the face of it, this looks like a good way to proceed. There are two ways, though, in which this procedure might fail. First, it might prove impossible to find a description on which most people can agree: in this case, the matching strategy will fail to produce a reasonable answer to Q3. Secondly, it might turn out that more than one suspect matches the description: in this case, the strategy will fail to produce a decisive answer.

A nice example of the matching strategy in action can be found in a paper by Roberts (1988). Roberts starts by listing the properties he takes instances of emotion to have (Roberts, 1988: 183–4). Here is a slightly simplified version of his list:

- In paradigm cases, instances of emotion are felt.
- They are intentional states.
- They are typically accompanied by physiological changes, some of which are felt.
- They typically depend on, but sometimes conflict with, our beliefs.
- Some types of emotion imply a disposition to behave in certain ways.
- Instances of emotion are sometimes, but not always, subject to voluntary control.
- They are typically experienced as unified states of mind, rather than as sets of components.

Roberts goes on to argue that emotional evaluations (as he understands them) have all the properties mentioned on his list. He concludes that instances of emotion are emotional evaluations.

We might wonder whether Roberts' approach will produce a *decisive* answer to Q3. On the face of it, his description is also compatible with the view that an instance of emotion is a complex process of some kind – for example, a combination of evaluation, desire and bodily feelings. Roberts, however, does not agree: he takes it that this kind of suggestion is ruled out by the last item on his list – the claim that emotions are typically experienced as *unified* states of mind. He takes this consideration to give strong support to the idea that instances of emotion are unitary phenomena, rather than complex responses (Roberts, 1988: 209). If he is right about this, it looks as if his list will at least exclude complex process theories of the kind proposed by Ekman and Goldie.

I am not convinced, though, that Roberts is right about this. I am happy to accept that emotional experience does have a certain seamless quality, at least while one is in its grip. But this does not entail that what is experienced is itself a unitary state. This is because there are other ways in which this feature of emotional experience could be explained. Plausibly, one important factor is the coherence of the emotional response: the fact that the subject's evaluation, attention, motivations and thoughts are all directed towards the same object and the same end. Another factor may be the intimate causal connections that exist between the different components of an emotional response – the way that feedback mechanisms, attentional focus, and so on, all work to ensure that the different components of the response tend to sustain and intensify each other. Arguably, then, it is the properties of the whole emotional response, rather than the emotional evaluation alone, that explain the unified quality of emotional experience (cf. Goldie, 2002: 247–8). If so, it looks as if Roberts' list is compatible with at least two different answers to Q3.

This, though, may be a problem with Roberts' list, rather than the matching strategy itself. It might be suggested that we could further refine or expand the list until we reach a single, decisive solution. This, though, prompts a further, more challenging objection: it is far from clear how we might set about this task.

As we have seen, the matching strategist's first task is to describe what an instance of emotion is like. It is important to notice that this is not the task that I took on in Chapter 1, when I described various kinds of emotional response. There I was trying to describe, in a general way, what happens when someone is angry or afraid. In other words, I was describing the subject's emotional response as a whole: I was not trying to describe the anger or fear *itself*. In contrast, the matching strategist needs to provide a description of the emotion *itself*, as distinct from its causes or effects. Moreover, the description must be one that most theorists could accept, even before they have agreed on an answer to Q3. This is a much more challenging task.

The nature of the challenge becomes clear when we consider some of the items on Roberts' list. Consider, for example, the distinction that Roberts makes between intentional states and bodily feelings: instances of emotion, he suggests, are *themselves* intentional states; bodily feelings merely *accompany* the emotion (Roberts, 1988: 207). This way of putting things is not uncontroversial. Why not say (as James might) that instances of emotions *themselves* have a bodily feel and that they are merely *accompanied by* intentional states? Or (as Ekman and Goldie would do) that bodily phenomenology and intentionality are both features of the emotion itself?

To be fair to Roberts, he does offer a reason for his claim that emotions are merely accompanied by bodily feelings. His reason is that bodily feelings are not *sufficient* for emotion: one can feel sick and tense, for example, without actually being anxious (Roberts, 1988: 189, n. 13). A supporter of James, I imagine, might want to protest that this does not take full account of the richness and diversity of bodily feelings, as James characterizes them. (For James, anxiety will involve not only feeling tense and sick, but also being aware of one's restless behaviour, the whine in one's voice, the urgent need to do something, and so on. It does not seem wholly unreasonable to think that *all* these feelings taken together might add up to a state of (objectless) anxiety.) For my current purposes, though, there is a more significant objection to press: even if Roberts is right to deny that bodily feelings alone can constitute an emotion, it does not follow that bodily feelings are merely associated with the emotion: they might yet be important *components* of the emotion.

Moreover (and this is the crucial point), it is not at all clear how we could *decide* this kind of question. Could we appeal to science? Empirical research might provide us with a detailed description of the properties of emotional responses and their components. But this will not help us to decide which of these properties belong to the emotion itself and which belong to its causes and effects. That is not an empirical question. What about our common-sense conception of emotion? Surprisingly, this does not seem to offer much help either. Admittedly, we seem to have a common-sense conception of what it means *to be afraid*: it involves taking oneself to be in danger; feeling agitated; having an urge to flee; and so on. But when it comes to deciding which of these things constitutes the emotion itself – as opposed to its accompaniments, causes or effects – common sense does not seem to offer much guidance. Should we say that fear itself has a bodily feel or that it is merely accompanied by bodily feelings? Should we say that a desire to flee is a component of fear or merely one of its effects? None of these possibilities, it seems to me, stands out as the common-sense view.

Why should this be? The reason, I want to suggest, has to do with the *complexity* of emotion. In Chapter 1, I suggested that emotional evaluations, feelings and motivations are not characteristically experienced in isolation, but rather come as a package. A consequence of this is that we can have a perfectly adequate conception of what is involved in being frightened without ever needing to make a distinction between the fear itself and the other phenomena that characteristically accompany it. We can understand why a frightened person feels, thinks and acts as they do without ever making this distinction.

If this is right, it constitutes a serious problem for the matching strategy: it is far from clear how we could generate an *uncontroversial* description of an instance of emotion. Without this, the matching strategy cannot produce a reasonable answer to Q3. It looks as if we should try a different approach.

William James: The Essentialist Strategy

An emotional response has many components. It is sometimes suggested, though, that one of these components is *essential* to an emotional response. In other words, the response will not count as an emotional response unless it includes a component of that kind. Theorists of emotion have sometimes appealed to this idea in order to support a particular answer to Q3. In fact, we have already met an example of this approach: James's argument for the view that instances of emotion are bodily feelings. As we saw in Chapter 2, James insists that bodily feelings are essential to emotion: without bodily feelings, the subject's response would not be a case of emotion at all. From this, he concludes that the bodily feelings constitute the emotion.

How promising is this strategy? To make his argument work, James needs to establish two things: (1) that cases of emotion *do* essentially involve bodily feelings and (2) that they have *no other* essential features. Neither of these tasks is likely to be straightforward. For one thing, it is not guaranteed that emotional responses have any essential ingredients at all. Moreover, bodily feelings are not the only possible candidate. As we have seen, Solomon holds that emotional evaluations are also essential to emotion (Solomon, 1973; see also Helm, 2001: 34). Indeed, it might be argued that emotional responses have essential structural or functional properties too. Of course, these suggestions are no more obviously correct than James's. My point is just that it is not a simple matter to decide what is or is not required for something to count as a case of emotion.

Still, it remains possible that, by carefully considering particular cases, we might establish that cases of emotion have certain essential components. Suppose, then, that we can do this. Would we then have a good answer to Q3? The answer, I want to suggest, is 'no'. In this case, the difficulty has nothing particularly to do with the nature of emotion. Rather, it relates to the essentialist strategy itself: the principle underlying the strategy looks weak. To see this, consider an analogous case.

The symptoms of smallpox are caused by a particular type of virus – *variola major*. People with smallpox develop a rash of papules: indeed, something will count as a case of ordinary smallpox (as opposed to another variant) only if the sufferer develops a rash of a particular kind. The sufferer will have other symptoms too: fever, headache, back pain and vomiting. These symptoms, though, are not essential: back pain and vomiting, in particular, are not always present. Hence a case of ordinary smallpox is likely to involve a range of symptoms – some essential, some non-essential, together with the viral infection that causes them.

So what constitutes the smallpox *itself*? There is more than one reasonable way to answer this question. One possibility is that we might identify the smallpox with the sufferer's symptoms. If we take this line, though, there seems to be no reason to identify the disease only with its essential symptoms – the rash, say; it would seem more natural to identify it with *all* the symptoms, essential and non-essential. Alternatively, we might identify the smallpox with the viral infection. On this view, the rash will be regarded as an essential *effect* of the disease, not as a component of the disease itself.

This is not a particularly unusual case. Complex artefacts often have a mix of essential and non-essential components: rice, for example, seems to be an essential ingredient of a risotto; still, the risotto does not consist only of the rice. Other things have essential causes or effects: there cannot be a footprint without a foot; still, the foot is an essential cause, not an essential component, of the print. Even if we could show, then, that bodily feelings are essential to emotion, it does not follow that the emotion consists only of those feelings: it might have other, non-essential components too. Indeed, it does not even follow that the bodily feelings are a component of the emotion at all: they might be an essential cause or effect.

Of course, if we could show that emotional responses have certain essential features, this would be an interesting and important discovery. It would certainly have a bearing on Q1 and Q2. But it would not help us to settle Q3.

Jesse Prinz: The Explanatory Strategy

I shall turn now to what I take to be the most promising of these three strategies. This is the approach taken by Prinz

(2004). Identifying an instance of emotion with a particular component, Prinz suggests, 'is a way of drawing attention to the feature that is most fundamental to understanding emotions' (Prinz, 2004: 18). I take it that what Prinz means is this: suppose that complex emotional responses include a particular component that plays a crucial role in explaining how the response develops. If so, we would have good reason to take this component to be the emotion. Arguably, this is precisely what we are doing when we identify an instance of smallpox with the viral infection: what makes the infection a good candidate to be the disease is that it plays a fundamental role in explaining why a case of smallpox develops as it does.

The success of the explanatory strategy depends on a particular empirical assumption – the assumption that there is a component of an emotional response that plays this crucial explanatory role. Prinz argues that emotional evaluations play this role: to explain why an emotional response develops as it does, he thinks, we need to focus on the intentional properties of the subject's evaluation: the subject responds as they do because they take the situation to be a certain way (Prinz, 2004: 55–67, 163).

I am happy to concede much of this. Nevertheless, I am not convinced that the explanatory strategy will yield a decisive answer to Q3. For, as I argued in Chapter 3, there are several ways in which we might explain why an emotional response takes the form that it does. In particular, we can also appeal to the functional properties of the response. Offering a functional explanation involves looking at the emotional response as a whole, in order to understand how its components work together to produce a particular outcome. The availability of this style of explanation might be taken to favour the view that an emotion is a complex process of some kind. Moreover, this top-down, functional explanation is not a rival to the intentional explanation suggested by Prinz. As we saw in Chapter 3, these two kinds of explanation might both be needed, depending on what we want to explain. If this is right, though, the explanatory strategy will generate two conflicting answers to Q3 – both equally defensible.

Prinz himself rejects the view that instances of emotion are complex processes (Prinz, 2004: 242). He asks us to compare a complex process theorist with someone who makes a similar claim about a visual experience, such as *seeing something red*. When someone sees something red, Prinz allows, they characteristically undergo other psychological changes – for example, they might focus their attention on the red thing, they might want to pick it up, and so on. Hence, visual experiences are not characteristically had in isolation, but within a broader psychological context. Nevertheless, as Prinz points out, there is no pressure to deny that visual experiences are simple psychological entities or to take them to include what we might otherwise think of as their further psychological effects.

On the picture of emotion I have been defending here, however, there is an important difference between the two cases. It is true that visual experiences characteristically occur within a wider psychological response. But this is not to say that they characteristically occur within a psychological response *of a specific kind* – one that has a particular kind of structure and function. How I respond to seeing something red will depend on the context. (Am I buying tomatoes or picking mushrooms, for example?) Owing to the many contexts in which such experiences may occur, it is worth picking them out as discrete states. In contrast, I have suggested, an emotional evaluation characteristically occurs in the context of a specific kind of psychological response – a complex emotional response, which has a particular function and which characteristically develops in a particular way – at least as far as its broad-brush features are concerned. Hence, picking on emotional evaluations as *the* fundamental emotional phenomenon draws our attention away from an equally fundamental aspect of emotion: the fact that emotional responses are processes that have a characteristic structure and function.

My argument here depends on a particular claim about the nature of emotional responses – that is, that they are coherent, organized responses with a recognizable structure and function. As I understand him, Prinz is sceptical about this. Nevertheless, in Chapter 3, I argued that there are reasons to take this claim seriously: emotional responses have certain features that are otherwise hard to explain. If that is right, we should also take seriously the possibility that the explanatory strategy will fail to yield a decisive answer to Q3: this is because there are at least two mutually compatible ways of explaining why an emotional response develops as it does.

Which Kind of Process?

A Problem about Diversity

I have considered three strategies that might be used to defend the view that an instance of emotion is identical with some particular component of an emotional response. I have argued that, if emotional responses have a complex and coherent structure which can be explained in functional terms, none of these strategies is likely to succeed. It might be suggested, then, that we should jump the other way, and take instances of emotion to be complex emotional responses. Certainly, views of this kind have some advantages: in particular, they take account of the complexity of emotional responses and the importance of their structural and functional properties. Even so, nothing I have said so far implies that we *should* adopt this kind of view, only that there is no decisive reason to reject it. Moreover, as we saw earlier, views of this kind prompt a question of their own. Given the diversity of emotional responses, why focus on one kind of process rather than another? Why, for example, pick on emotional reactions rather than emotional attitudes, or emotional attitudes rather than emotional reactions?[5]

Ekman supports his account by appealing to a close cousin of the essentialist strategy: he suggests that identifying instances of emotion with brief emotional reactions captures everything that is *distinctive* of emotion (Ekman 1992: 195). In contrast, emotional attitudes might be thought to lack some of these features – for example, they do not involve physiological or expressive changes; or, more precisely, they involve them only insofar as they involve emotional reactions. It is not clear, though, that emotional reactions include *everything* that is distinctive of emotion. Emotional attitudes can involve long-term changes to the subject's motivations and priorities; they can involve extended processes of thought, which do not have time to develop during a brief emotional reaction: arguably, these are distinctively emotional phenomena too. Moreover, like the essentialist strategy, this seems to be a weak principle to use. We can see this if we consider the smallpox example again. Presumably, the rash that defines ordinary smallpox distinguishes cases of ordinary smallpox from cases of other kinds; but this does not seem to be a reason to identify ordinary smallpox with the rash.

A better option for Ekman might be to employ the explanatory strategy. He might argue, against Prinz, that it is the shape of an emotional reaction that determines how emotional episodes or attitudes develop. Even if this were true, however, Ekman would face the same problem as Prinz: if the coherence claim is correct, there are other, compatible ways to explain how emotional episodes and attitudes develop. Functional, intentional and narrative considerations are all likely to come into play – considerations that may well be thought to favour other kinds of answer to Q3.

A Pluralist Solution?

Perhaps a possible solution is to adopt a *pluralist* account. In other words, we might insist that emotional reactions, episodes and attitudes can all be regarded as instances of emotion. Indeed, some form of pluralism might be thought to offer the best chance of explaining what people ordinarily mean when they use terms such as 'anger' or 'fear' to refer to particular psychological occurrences. For example, consider the following sentence:

'Igor's triumph was short-lived.'

We could imagine someone using this sentence to describe a brief reaction; but it might equally be used to describe an enduring attitude. Hence, in some contexts, the implication might be that Igor's triumph faded almost immediately; in others, that his triumph faded after only a few weeks.

Earlier, however, I suggested that in investigating Q3, we are looking for an answer that will be helpful in developing a theory of emotion. It is far from clear that pluralism will provide this. Once again, the difficulty stems from the diversity of emotion. I have suggested that emotional reactions, episodes and attitudes are interestingly different kinds of response, and that, in discussing certain questions about emotion, it often matters which kind of response we have in mind. Gathering emotional reactions, episodes and attitudes together under a single label runs the risk of blurring the distinctions between them, and so overlooking the richness and variety of emotional phenomena. Theorists such as Goldie and Ekman have resisted adopting a pluralistic view, partly because (I take it) they have recognized the need to distinguish *between* different kinds of emotional response. I agree that the distinction is well worth drawing. Where I disagree is over the suggestion that one kind of response has more claim than another to be viewed as an instance of emotion.

An Alternative Approach

I have been arguing that a principled answer to Q3 may be very hard to find. My argument is far from decisive: in particular, there may be other strategies that might be used. Nonetheless, it does seem to me to be worth considering the possibility that, as theorists of emotion, we might do better to call off the search. In particular, it is not obvious that very much would be lost by doing this. As theorists of emotion, we can manage perfectly well without an answer to Q3. Instead, we can simply embrace the idea that there is a rich variety of phenomena to be investigated – reactions, episodes, attitudes, evaluations, feelings, thoughts, desires, actions and more – all of which have equal title to be thought of as emotional phenomena. There are plenty of questions we can ask about these various phenomena without having to worry about which of them should be honoured with the title '*the* emotion'. My positive proposal, then, is that we might simply decide to put Q3 to one side, and instead focus our attention on emotional phenomena, in all their richness and diversity. That, at least, is what I propose to do in what follows.

Classifying Emotions

Classificatory Questions

In what remains of this chapter, I shall turn my attention to two other ways of understanding the question 'What is an emotion?'

> Q1   What it makes it right to classify a certain type of response (contempt, say) as an *emotional* response and not, say, as a mood or a bodily sensation?

> Q2   How should we distinguish between different *types* of emotional response? What is the difference, for example, between contempt and anger?

There is more than one kind of objective that someone might have in raising these questions. One possibility is that they are trying to provide a detailed account of everyday talk about emotion. Arguably, this is a project that requires a book to itself: as Roddy Cowie (2010) points out, the ways in which people describe and classify emotional phenomena in everyday situations are surprisingly subtle, diverse and hard to pin down. Moreover, capturing everyday usage seems to be more a matter for empirical research than philosophical analysis. Alternatively, the aim might be to develop a well-defined taxonomy of emotion for some specific theoretical purpose. It is not clear, though, that my discussion here would benefit from this. Instead, what I would like to do is to explore, in a relatively abstract and open-ended way, three considerations to which theorists of emotion have often appealed in classifying emotional phenomena; in particular, I want to consider how they relate to each other.

In discussing this issue, I shall return once again to the themes introduced in Chapter 3. Indeed, these issues provide a further opportunity to consider how we might appeal to the structure and function of an emotional response in developing a theory of emotion.

Classifying Emotions: Three Considerations

I shall start by investigating Q2. In particular, I shall focus on *complex* emotional responses – reactions, episodes and attitudes. How might we go about distinguishing between, say, an angry attitude and one of contempt; or between an episode of embarrassment and an episode of shame?

One possibility is that we might focus on their *phenomenal character* – the way that they feel. A proponent of this kind of account need not focus wholly on bodily feelings. As I suggested in Chapter 1, the feel of an emotional response is determined not only by its physiological and behavioural ingredients, but also by its psychological elements, particularly changes to attention and motivation.

A second possibility is that we could classify emotional responses according to their *intentional* properties. On this suggestion, anger and contempt constitute different types of emotion because they involve different kinds of evaluation: an angry evaluation is concerned with offence and motivates the subject to retaliate; while a contemptuous evaluation represents its object as inferior or worthless and motivates the subject to withdraw.

A third possibility is that we might appeal to the *structure* and *function* of an emotional response. Angry reactions, episodes and attitudes, it might be suggested, involve a similar pattern of evaluation, attention and motivation: the subject registers that someone is behaving offensively, their attention switches to the situation and they are motivated to retaliate. Angry reactions, episodes and attitudes share a function too – to enable the subject to deal with offence. Contempt, in contrast, involves a different kind of evaluation and a different set of motivations; its function relates to a different kind of situation. It might be suggested, then, that anger and contempt constitute different types of emotion because they differ in structure and function.

Functional/structural accounts are sometimes associated with a further claim: that we can identify a precise (and relatively small) number of 'basic emotions'. Ekman (1992) is the best-known advocate of this view in recent years. As we saw earlier, he holds that instances of emotion are (something like) emotional reactions. These, he suggests, can be typed by their structure and function. Moreover, he argues, there are just a few types of emotional reaction: he lists anger, fear, enjoyment, sadness, disgust, surprise, and perhaps contempt, shame, guilt, embarrassment and awe. He leaves room, though, for finer distinctions. In particular, he suggests that each basic emotion can be viewed as a *family*, with several members: frustration, indignation and rage, for example, all belong to the anger family. On Ekman's account, though, love, grief, sexual jealousy and envy do not count as types of emotion: they are more complex psychological phenomena, which involve several different types of emotional reaction.

It is worth noting, though, that a functional/structural theorist is not forced to adopt this kind of view. Indeed, even if Ekman is right to claim that there are just a few types of emotional reaction, this need not imply that there are just a few types of emotional episode or attitude. Suppose, for example, that he is right to think that an episode of sexual jealousy does not involve a distinctive type of jealous reaction, but rather a mix of angry, fearful and sad reactions. A functional/structural theorist might yet insist that episodes of sexual jealousy involve a distinctive pattern of evaluation, motivation and attention, which can be discerned only when we look at the episode as a whole. Moreover, they might argue, an episode of sexual jealousy functions as a response to a specific kind of situation – one involving the infidelity of a sexual partner. If so, we might well have reason to take sexual jealousy to be a type of emotion – albeit of a more complex kind than anger or fear.

Indeed, it looks as if all three accounts can allow for a degree of flexibility in how we categorize emotional responses. This is because function, structure, intentional content and phenomenal character can all be specified in more or less detail. Hence all these accounts leave room for more or less fine-grained distinctions between types of emotional response.

A Happy Convergence?

It is not obvious that we need to choose between these accounts. Certainly, the functional/structural account and the intentional account seem to overlap. Moreover, in Chapter 6, I am going to endorse a *teleosemantic* theory of intentional content. According to a teleosemantic theory, the content of an emotional evaluation *depends* on the structure and function of the emotional response that it is supposed to prompt. On this approach, then, these two accounts are effectively equivalent. For this reason, I have no need to choose between them.

The structure of an emotional response and its phenomenal character will also be closely related: the feel of an angry response will be determined, in part, by the kinds of psychological change that the functional/structural theorist takes to be distinctive of anger. In this second case, however, the fit is not quite perfect. This is because the functional/structural account emphasizes the psychological aspects of anger; but the phenomenal character of anger is determined by its physiological and behavioural aspects too.

For human beings, these different aspects of an emotional response will tend to coincide. As Bennett Helm has pointed out, however, it is possible to imagine cases where they come apart (Helm, 2009: 254). (To elaborate on his example) imagine meeting members of an alien race whose response to offence is in many ways just like ours: in particular, they respond with a similar pattern of evaluation, attention and motivation. Nevertheless, their bodies, and therefore their behaviour, are quite different: rather than clenching their fists, they wave their tentacles; rather than frowning, they extend their eye-stalks; and so on. It is a good bet, then, that their offence-response does not *feel* to them quite as anger does to us. Should their offence-response be classified as anger? The functional/structural account implies that it should. The phenomenal account implies that it should not.

My own inclination is to say that these alien creatures *do* respond to offence with anger, even if their angry feelings are not the same as ours. This is not to say that the phenomenal character of an emotional experience is unimportant: in particular, it plays a role in helping people to identify their emotions. But to understand why the situation has elicited this response, to predict how the response is likely to develop, and to make sense of the subject's behaviour, we need to appeal to its functional, structural and intentional properties.

For this reason, it seems to me, these properties play a particularly fundamental role in determining what kind of response this is.

This is, admittedly, a fanciful case. But we could raise a similar question in relation to non-human animals. Do orangutans experience anger? Do dolphins? Do cows? Do squid? I am not sure how to answer these questions. But I take it that the matter is not decided *simply* by the consideration that the bodies – and so, presumably, the bodily feelings – of these creatures differ from ours. Functional and structural similarities, it seems to me, carry more weight than differences in phenomenal character.

Classifying Components

What should we say about the *components* of complex emotional responses – angry evaluations, thoughts or feelings, say? These, I take it, count as angry phenomena simply because they are components of angry reactions, episodes or attitudes. Indeed, many of these phenomena characteristically occur only as part of an angry response. This is true of angry feelings, for example. For this reason, it might make sense to describe such a feeling as an angry feeling, even if – as the result of some neural malfunction, say – it were to occur in isolation. But this is not true of every component. Consider the thought 'He did that on purpose!' This thought might well occur within an angry episode; but it might equally occur within an episode of fear, happiness or admiration, or as a calm assessment of the situation. In the latter cases, we can hardly describe it as an angry thought. But it makes sense to do so in the first case: in doing this, we locate it within a particular kind of psychological process, helping us to explain why it occurred on this occasion and to predict its likely effects.

The Boundaries of Emotion

I have suggested that the functional and structural features of emotional phenomena have a particularly important role to play in classifying them into types. Arguably, these features have an equally significant role to play in answering Q1 – that is, in distinguishing emotional phenomena from other kinds of psychological phenomena.

Here, for example, is one set of features that might be thought to capture the distinctive character of an emotional response:

- Responses of these types function to deal with a specific kind of challenge or opportunity – of a kind that need not be restricted to the subject's own body, but can involve features of the subject's physical and social environment.
- Responses of these types characteristically involve an evaluation of the situation and changes to attention and motivation.
- Responses of these types characteristically involve further cognitive, behavioural and physiological changes.
- Characteristically, responses of these types are felt.

Certainly, these features seem to be shared by many types of emotion. Moreover, it looks as if we could appeal to these features to distinguish emotions from other kinds of psychological phenomena. Consider, for example, bodily sensations, such as hunger or nausea. These states are similar to emotions in some ways: they tend to involve changes to attention and motivation and they are characteristically felt. But bodily sensations are never responses to situations in the subject's *environment*: they are concerned only with changes in the subject's own body.

Emotions can also be contrasted with moods. Some theorists of emotion deny that there is a clear distinction between moods and emotions. In particular, it is sometimes suggested that moods are very *general* emotions: to be irritable, for example, is to be angry about things in general; to be apprehensive is to be frightened about things in general (Solomon, 1993 [1976]: 71; Goldie, 2000: 17). Certainly, moods seem to have many features in common with emotion: arguably, they involve an evaluation of the situation and various cognitive and physiological changes; and they have a phenomenal character. However, I have argued elsewhere (Price, 2006b) that there is a difference in *function* between an emotion and a mood. Moods, I take it, are states of vigilance: they prompt the subject to look out for a particular kind of situation and prime them to respond in a particular way should it arise. Someone who is irritable, for example, is on the look-out for offence, and primed to respond with anger. Anger, in contrast, is a response to a *particular* offence – one that has actually happened or is about to happen.

We might conclude, then, that emotional responses share certain functional and structural properties that distinguish them from other psychological phenomena. Nevertheless, some caveats are required. On the one hand, there seem to be emotions that lack some of the properties I listed above. One example is hope: hope is usually categorized as an emotion; and it has many of the properties that I listed. On the face of it, though, hope does not involve motivational changes: the hopeful subject is not motivated to *do* anything; they can only wait and see. Perhaps the most we can say is that hope functions to forestall certain motivational changes, ensuring that the subject remains open to a certain possibility, rather than giving up and moving on.[6]

Conversely, there are some types of psychological response that seem to fit the description given above but which are not obviously types of emotion. Consider, for example, the case of sexual desire, where this is understood as desire for a particular person. Arguably, the function of sexual desire is to ensure that the subject takes advantage of a specific opportunity for sexual activity with an attractive partner; it characteristically involves an evaluation of its object as sexually attractive; it involves changes to attention and motivation – not to mention thoughts, imaginings and physiological changes; and it has a phenomenal character. Yet, for me at least, sexual desire is not naturally classed as an emotion, though I find it hard to say exactly why.[7]

There are, then, reasons to suppose that the term 'emotion' does not pick out a neatly defined class of psychological phenomena. While emotions tend to share certain functional and structural features, there are unusual and borderline cases. As Amélie Rorty puts it, in a now much-quoted phrase, emotions do not form a 'natural class' (Rorty, 1980: 1).

Nevertheless, we might still think that the description I gave earlier has some use: it characterizes, more or less, the phenomena that we tend to categorize as emotions; and it draws our attention to the different ways in which these phenomena tend to resemble each other and differ from psychological phenomena of other kinds. For some theoretical purposes it might well be necessary to develop a more careful and principled taxonomy – one that might force us to revise our everyday classifications (Griffiths, 1997). For my present purposes, though, I have no need to insist on anything more precise.

Summary

In this chapter, I have considered three different versions of the question 'What is an emotion?' None of the answers I have given have been straightforward. Indeed, in the case of Q3, I argued that it may be impossible to find a good answer. This need not worry us, I suggested, because we do not need to answer Q3 in order to develop a theory of emotion.

In the case of Q2, I argued that the functional and structural properties of emotional phenomena have a particularly important role to play. Still, on the account of intentional content that I shall present in Chapter 6, the intentional features of an emotional response will necessarily reflect its functional and structural features. In the case of human beings, at least, this is characteristically true of phenomenal features too. But when this is not the case, there are good reasons to give more weight to functional and structural considerations.

Finally, I suggested that we might be able to answer Q1 by appealing to the functional and structural properties shared by different types of emotion. It is possible to construct a profile that fits most types of emotion and distinguishes them from other psychological states such as bodily sensations and moods. To do this, though, is not to give necessary and sufficient conditions for being an emotion: unusual and borderline cases remain.

Further Reading

For a helpful discussion of the debate over Q3, see Prinz (2004: Chap. 1). For some different answers to Q3, see James (1890: Chap. 25); Roberts (1988); Goldie (2000: Chap. 1); Prinz (2004: Chaps 1 and 3). Many theorists identify instances of emotion with particular components of the emotional response. They include Shaffer (1983); Solomon (1993 [1976]: Chap. 5); Nussbaum (2001: Chap. 1); Helm (2009); Whiting (2011). For another complex process theory, see Robinson (2005: Chap. 3). For some views about the classification of emotion, see Ekman (1992); Griffiths (1997: esp. Chap. 9); Roberts (2003: Chap. 3). Cowie (2010) offers an interesting account of how emotions are categorized in everyday talk.

4
What Is an Emotional Evaluation?

Introduction

Zack lets the library door slam: Alice bristles with anger. Alice's angry response involves a particular *evaluation* of Zack's behaviour: her reaction implies that she represents Zack's behaviour as an offence. When she realizes that Zack is, in fact, struggling with a pile of heavy books, her evaluation of the situation changes and her anger fades away.

The remaining four chapters of this book are all concerned, in different ways, with emotional evaluations. In particular, I am concerned with the evaluations that initiate and sustain our emotional responses. I shall begin, in this chapter, by considering what *kinds* of state these are: are they *judgements*, for example? In Chapter 6, I shall investigate their intentional content: what are emotional evaluations about? In Chapters 7 and 8, I shall be concerned with some different ways in which these states can be evaluated – as rational or irrational, authentic or inauthentic, and so on. In Chapter 7, in particular, I shall return to some of the questions discussed here. Indeed, the issue raised in this chapter will not be fully resolved until then.

An emotional evaluation is an intentional state: it is about a certain object or situation, and it represents that object or situation as being a certain way. It is important to bear in mind, though, that the intentionality of an emotional response is a complex matter. This is because emotional responses include at least three different kinds of intentional state:

- the evaluation or evaluations that initiate and sustain the response;
- the perceptions, thoughts, memories, imaginings and desires that arise in the course of the response;
- emotional feelings: that is, perceptions of the bodily and psychological changes that help to constitute the response.

Moreover, as we saw in Chapter 2, both Prinz (2004) and Solomon (2003b) suggest that emotional feelings can take on a further function: they can signal that the subject is facing an emotionally significant situation. In making this claim, Solomon and Prinz both have bodily feelings in mind; I shall suggest later on, though, that this point might well apply to non-bodily feelings too. This raises the possibility that we might think of emotional feelings as themselves embodying a kind of evaluation of the situation – one that might influence the subject's subsequent beliefs and desires, for example.

An emotional response, then, might involve several different kinds of intentional state, any of which might reasonably be described as an 'emotional evaluation'. In what follows, however, I want to focus on just one kind of intentional state: the evaluations that initiate and sustain the response. It will be important in what follows, then, to distinguish these evaluations from the other intentional states that I have mentioned. In particular, I want to maintain a distinction between the emotional *experience*, which arises *as a result* of the bodily and psychological changes involved in an emotional response, and the evaluations that *initiate* those changes. To keep this clear, I shall henceforth refer to the latter as 'emotional evaluations$_i$'. (The subscripted 'i' is there as a reminder that it is an *initiating* evaluation that I have in mind.)

As I have said, it is emotional evaluations$_i$ that interest me here. This is not because I think that there is nothing interesting to say about the intentionality of emotional feelings or about the role of thought and imagination within an emotional response. Still, I think that there are some important questions about emotion that can be answered only by getting clear about the nature of states that initiate emotional responses. When is it fitting to become afraid, or envious or indignant? What do our emotional responses tell us about the world? Can we educate our emotional susceptibilities? Answering these questions means understanding how, and under what circumstances, emotional responses are supposed to be produced; and this means understanding the evaluations, that initiate our emotional responses – what kind of states these are and what they are about. Moreover, as I hope will become clearer as we go on, there are some issues about the rationality of emotion that depend on how our emotional responses are produced.

Still, not all theorists have drawn such an explicit distinction between emotional evaluations, and the experiences that emerge out of an emotional response. For this reason, it is not always entirely clear how their views bear on the question that I have in mind here. In what follows, I shall usually begin by assuming that the theorists whom I discuss are concerned with emotional evaluations, rather than emotional feelings. As we shall see, though, I shall sometimes need to qualify or abandon this assumption.

As we saw in Chapter 2, theorists of emotion disagree about the nature of emotional evaluations. Robert Solomon (1993 [1976], 2003a [1988]) and Martha Nussbaum (2001) argue that they are evaluative judgements, while some other theorists have identified them with beliefs or perhaps complexes of belief and desire (see, e.g., Lyons, 1980; Marks, 1982; Shaffer, 1983; Nash, 1989). In contrast, Goldie argues that emotional responses involve a distinct class of intentional state, 'feelings towards', which, he suggests, are similar to perceptions in some ways. In recent years, the idea that emotional evaluations, can be compared to perceptions has become increasingly popular; indeed, some theorists have suggested that these states *are* perceptions of some kind.[1]

In this chapter, I shall examine this dispute. I shall begin, in the following section, by explaining what I take judgements, beliefs and perceptions to be. In the third section, I shall investigate some objections to the claim that emotional evaluations, are judgements or beliefs: I shall argue that there is at least one strong reason to reject this view. In the final section, I shall consider the suggestion that emotional evaluations, are, or are importantly similar to, perceptions.

Judgements, Beliefs and Perceptions

Judgements and Beliefs

According to Solomon, a judgement is a kind of mental *act* – the act of forming a belief (Solomon, 2003a [1988]: 110–12). Admittedly, this definition does not seem to apply to what Solomon calls 'judgements of the body' (Solomon, 2003b: 191–2): as Solomon describes it, a 'judgement of the body' does not involve forming a belief, but rather becoming aware of one's own bodily reaction to the situation. For this reason, I shall set 'judgements of the body' to one side for now. At this point, I want to focus on Solomon's narrower definition, which relates judgements to beliefs. What, though, is a belief? For reasons that will become clear, this is not an easy question to answer. I shall begin by offering an initial account, which I shall then need to qualify.

I believe that piranhas eat meat. My belief represents a certain state of affairs (piranhas eating meat); and it represents it as *being the case.* In this respect, a belief contrasts with a desire – for example, my desire to keep piranhas as pets. My desire also represents a certain state of affairs (my having some pet piranhas); but it does not represent it as *being the case*, but rather as a goal *to be achieved.* Desires and beliefs do have some properties in common: they both function to direct our behaviour; and they do this, very often, by contributing to processes of practical reasoning. However, they do this in different ways: the job of a desire is to motivate us to pursue a particular goal or to engage in a particular activity; the job of a belief is to represent how things are, so ensuring that we pursue our goals in ways that are appropriate to the situation.

This is not the whole story, however. It ignores an important distinction – the distinction between evaluative and non-evaluative beliefs. Suppose that I believe that piranhas are impressive creatures. This is an *evaluative* belief: it involves taking piranhas to have a certain kind of value – one that calls for admiration or respect. In contrast, my belief that piranhas eat meat is a *non-evaluative* belief: I can believe this without regarding piranhas as having any particular value, either positive or negative. The distinction between evaluative and non-evaluative beliefs is profoundly controversial. The controversy turns on issues about the metaphysics of value that I cannot hope to settle here. Still, I shall try to say *something* about the difference between these two kinds of belief. Rather than trying to tackle the metaphysical question, I shall flag up a difference in their psychological roles.

The account of belief that I gave earlier implied a sharp division between belief and desire. In the case of non-evaluative beliefs, this seems roughly right. In the case of evaluative beliefs, however, the contrast between belief and desire is less clear-cut. Admittedly, evaluative beliefs do not seem to *be* desires: my belief that piranhas are impressive creatures need not motivate me to behave in any particular way. Nevertheless, as Solomon implies, our evaluative judgements and beliefs do seem to be *bound up* with our desires in some sense. The things that we value are the things that matter to us – things that we may be inclined to want to foster, or defend, or uphold. For this reason, it seems plausible that evaluative beliefs can, by themselves, be *sources* of desire.

Suppose, for example, that I want to see piranhas in the wild, or to campaign for their preservation. On the face of it, my belief that piranhas are impressive animals is enough, by itself, to explain why I want these things. In contrast, my belief that piranhas eat meat can influence my desires; but *how* it does so depends on the desires and values that I already have. It is not by itself a source of desire. This link between evaluative judgements and desires may well explain why theorists such as Solomon and Nussbaum have found it natural to identify emotional evaluations with evaluative rather than non-evaluative judgements: for emotional responses characteristically involve changes to motivation and, in some cases, an urge for immediate action.

Perceptions

When I use the term 'perception', what I have in mind is a perceptual *experience*. Examples might include seeing an aubergine as purple, hearing someone's voice as husky, or tasting a ripe mango as sweet. These are all perceptions of objects and features in the environment. In what follows, I shall refer to these as *external sense perceptions*. As we have seen, though, bodily feelings – hunger or pain, for example – might also be regarded as perceptions: they are perceptions of changes in our bodies. As we saw in Chapter 2, William James characterizes bodily feelings in this way, and I shall do the same in what follows.

Like judgements and beliefs, perceptions represent objects and events as being a certain way. They also play a crucial role in guiding behaviour. They can do this *indirectly*, by grounding judgements about how things are. But they can also guide behaviour *directly*: seeing how big the cup is, for example, I unconsciously adjust my grip to match. Finally, it might be thought that some kinds of perceptual experience can actually motivate behaviour: the pain of a burnt finger, for example, motivates me to nurse the injury. This raises the possibility that we might think of pain as an *evaluative* perception – one that not only signals that the body has been damaged in some way, but also presents the damage as something *bad*. There is room for dispute about this last suggestion. An alternative view is that pain involves two separate components: a perceptual component that registers the bodily damage; and a separate, motivational element – a valence marker, perhaps. I shall not take a stand on this here.

Perceptions, then, have some properties in common with judgements and beliefs. How, though, do they differ? In the next section, I shall present three contrasts between perceptions and beliefs or judgements. They are certainly not the only contrasts that could be drawn. But they are the ones that will be most important in what follows.

Contrasting Perception and Belief

Phenomenology

Perceptual experiences have a rich phenomenology: hard though it is to capture in words, there is something it is like to see an aubergine as purple or to taste the sweetness of a ripe mango. Moreover, each individual experience has a *specific* phenomenal character: the experience of seeing something as purple is not at all like the experience of tasting something as sweet.

Is there something it is like to judge that aubergines are purple, or to believe that mangos are sweet? This is a highly controversial issue.[2] Certainly it does seem plausible that there is something it is like to make up one's mind about something. It is less clear, though, that each particular judgement has a specific phenomenal character – that there is something it is like to judge that aubergines are purple, as opposed to, say, judging that mangoes are sweet. In making these judgements, perhaps, I might entertain certain mental images or formulate certain words in my head; arguably, though, the act of judging in each case feels the same. Whatever we say about these issues, we can at least be sure that judgements and perceptual experiences do not have the *same* kind of phenomenal character. Judging that an aubergine is purple is not like seeing it as purple.

Responsiveness to reasoning

Some judgements and beliefs are products of conscious reasoning or inference. Suppose that I discover my house keys in the dishwasher. Working out how they got there might involve a complex train of reasoning: there might be a number of clues to consider; and I might have to weigh up the evidence with care. If I am still uncertain, I might decide to suspend judgement, and look for more evidence. In other cases, as Solomon (2003a [1988]) points out, we form judgements immediately and unreflectively: I taste the sweetness in the mango, and immediately judge that it is ripe; a neighbour's face strikes me as open and honest, and I immediately judge her to be trustworthy. Even in these cases, though, our judgements generally remain *responsive* or *sensitive* to reasoning: they can be revised in the light of new evidence or further thought. If I discover that my neighbour has had a long career as a confidence trickster, I might well revise my assumption that she can be trusted with my bank details; at the very least, I might suspend judgement.

In contrast, perceptual experiences are never produced by conscious reasoning or inference. The processes that generate our perceptual experiences are unconscious and automatic: things just strike us as being a particular way. Moreover, perceptions are not responsive to reasoning in the way that judgements are. Suppose, for example, that I am looking at a toy spade that has been left in a paddling pool, half-submerged in the water. The spade's handle looks crooked to me. But I do not *believe* that the handle is crooked: its crooked appearance, I think, is due to the refraction of light. Even so, the handle will continue to *look* crooked. It is not difficult to find other examples of this phenomenon: when people disembark from a boat, they often feel as if they are still bobbing up and down, even though they know they are not; as an ambulance races past, I hear the pitch of the siren change, even though I know that this is a case of the Doppler effect. Further examples can be found in the literature on optical illusions. Consider, for example, the much-cited Müller–Lyer illusion (Figure 1): for many people, the two lines look different lengths, even after they have confirmed with a ruler that they are not. In all these cases, the subject's perceptual experience persists, even though they know that it is misleading. This is not to deny that people can sometimes exercise *indirect* control over how things look or sound to them: if I want to see the spade handle as straight, for example, I can try looking at it from a different angle. We should say, perhaps, that perceptions are not *directly* responsive to reasoning, in the way that judgements are.

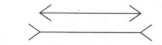

Figure 1: The Müller–Lyer illusion

Rationality

Judgements and beliefs answer to *norms of rationality*: they are supposed to be based on reasons and to be consistent with each other. Suppose, for example, that I am convinced that my son put my keys in the dishwasher. To say that my belief is rational implies that I have some good reason to hold it; if I realize that I have no evidence to support my belief, and yet continue to hold it, then my belief is irrational. Again, suppose that I believe not only that my son put the keys in the dishwasher but also that he was not in the house at the time; and that I insist on both these things for some time, even though it is obvious that they cannot both be true. In this case, too, my beliefs seem to be irrational. I should either drop one of them or suspend belief until I can decide between them.

In contrast, we do not characterize perceptions as rational or irrational. Admittedly, when I see the spade handle as crooked, my visual experience *conflicts* with my judgement: my perception and my judgement cannot both be right. Still, this does not seem to be a case of irrationality. My experience is misleading, perhaps, but there is nothing illogical or absurd about my continuing to have it.

In this section, I have identified three contrasts between judgements and perceptions: they have different phenomenal properties; they are produced by different kinds of psychological process; and they are judged by different norms. Recognizing these differences can help us to understand what is at stake in the dispute about emotional evaluations₁. On the one hand, we might think of emotional evaluations₁ as judgements or beliefs – states that are directly responsive to reasoning and which can be evaluated in rational terms. On the other hand, we might regard them as more like perceptual experiences – states that are only indirectly responsive to reasoning and which are not evaluated by the standards of rationality. In the next section, I shall consider two objections to the claim that emotional evaluations₁ are judgements. As we have seen, this claim is not exactly equivalent to the claim that emotional evaluations₁ are beliefs. However, similar objections can be levelled at the belief view too.

Emotional Evaluations₁ as Judgements

The Objection from Phenomenology

One objection that is sometimes made to the judgement view is that it gives the wrong account of the phenomenal character of emotion. In particular, the objection goes, it fails to recognize that the phenomenal and intentional features of emotion are inextricably linked.

It seems undeniable that emotional responses have a phenomenal character; it seems undeniable, too, that the phenomenal character of an emotional response differs from the phenomenal character of a judgement. Judgement theorists often try to account for this by suggesting that emotion involves a combination of judgement and feeling. Indeed, as we saw in Chapter 2, Solomon (2003a [1988], 2003b) makes a suggestion of just this kind. It has been objected, though, that this approach is inadequate: it treats the phenomenal character of emotion as a kind of 'add on' or afterthought, with very little explanatory work to do (Goldie, 2000: 40).

Michelle Montague (2009) has presented a particularly careful version of this objection (see also Gunther 2004). As we shall see, however, it is not altogether clear how her argument bears on the question that I am addressing here. This is because Montague's argument is concerned with the claim that *instances of emotion* are judgements. In contrast, I am concerned with the claim that *emotional evaluations* are judgements. It is not immediately obvious, then, that we are talking about the same thing. Before considering this, however, we first need to set out Montague's argument.

To appreciate Montague's point, it helps to start from a case of perception. Imagine someone hearing the hum of a bumble bee nearby: on the face of it, there is just one thing here – an auditory experience, which both presents the bee as being a certain way (humming nearby) and has a certain phenomenal character (loud and buzzy, perhaps). It would seem rather odd to insist that there are really two things: an auditory representation of the bee nearby, accompanied by a loud and buzzy sensation. Rather, the auditory experience represents the bee as humming nearby in virtue of being a loud and buzzy sensation. The same thing, Montague thinks, is true of emotion: embarrassment (say) represents the situation as awkward just in virtue of feeling embarrassing. An instance of emotion, she concludes, is not a judgement plus a set of feelings. Rather, it is similar to a perceptual experience, in that its phenomenal and intentional features cannot be pulled apart (cf. Döring, 2003: 226).

What is the best way to interpret Montague's argument? Should we take it to cast light on the nature of emotional evaluations$_i$? Or is it concerned with some other component of the emotional response? The answer depends on what kinds of phenomenal properties Montague has in mind. A clue comes when she describes the phenomenal character of sadness. She writes: 'There is something it is like to *feel* sad, both psychically and physically – perhaps for some it is a kind of feeling of vulnerability and melancholy weariness accompanied by bodily fatigue' (Montague, 2009: 183). It is not immediately obvious how to interpret this. One possibility is that what Montague has in mind are the feelings produced by the various changes – bodily and psychological – that help to constitute the sad response. Bodily fatigue, certainly, seems to fall into this category. If so, however, the point she is making does not concern emotional evaluations$_i$, but rather the emotional *experience* generated once the emotional response is underway.

Certainly, there is no reason to doubt that the emotional experience, taken as a whole, has a rich phenomenology. Moreover, as I mentioned earlier, it might be thought that the emotional experience can itself constitute a kind of evaluation of the situation. We have already met the suggestion, made by Solomon and Prinz, that the bodily feelings characteristic of fear might themselves constitute a way of recognizing that one is in danger. If bodily feelings can play this role, there is no obvious reason to deny that this might be true of the emotional experience as a whole. If so, we could certainly make sense of the idea that an emotional response involves a kind of evaluation – an emotional experience – whose intentional features are intimately connected with its phenomenal character, just as Montague describes.

It is important to notice, though, that it would be quite possible for someone to endorse this view of emotional *experiences*, while insisting that emotional *evaluations$_i$* – the evaluations that *initiate* emotional responses – are evaluative judgements. Someone who took this view would hold that our emotional experiences, though not themselves evaluative judgements, are ultimately dependent on them. This account of emotional experience, then, does not undermine the judgement view, where this is understood as an account of emotional evaluations$_i$.

There is, though, a second possibility. The claim might be that emotional evaluations$_i$ *themselves* have a distinctive phenomenal character. What, though, might this be? For a promising suggestion, we might go back to Aristotle: our emotional responses, Aristotle suggests, are bound up with pleasure and pain: to be angry, for example, is to be *pained* by offence (*Nicomachean Ethics*, 1105b21; cf. Helm, 2009; see also Greenspan, 1988: 30–5). This is not, of course, a physical pain: we might compare it, rather, to the pain of hearing metal scraping on glass; or of encountering a particularly awful pun. (Montague's 'melancholy weariness' might be read as referring to a psychological pain of this kind.) Nor is it the same as experiencing the angry response *itself* as painful: some people seem to enjoy the experience of anger, though they are nonetheless aggrieved by the offence. Moreover, as Bennett Helm has pointed out (Helm, 2009: 249), to feel pleasure or pain at something is a way of *evaluating* it: it is to represent it, in a very basic way, as good or bad.

Moreover, there is a further factor we might consider. I have suggested that some types of emotional response – fear and anger, say – involve urges to act in particular ways. Arguably, these urges are components of the evaluations$_i$ themselves. (Indeed, in Chapter 6, I shall argue that they are.) If so, these urges will also help to determine the phenomenal character of angry and fearful evaluations$_i$, for, after all, these urges are felt.

It might be suggested, then, that an angry evaluation$_i$ itself has a distinctive phenomenal character: it is aggrieved and vengeful. As it happens, I think that this suggestion is a plausible one; moreover, it gives us some sense of what an emotional evaluation$_i$ might be like, if it is not a judgement. An alternative picture, though, does not in itself amount to an objection to the judgement view: we need a reason to prefer the alternative proposal. It might be argued, perhaps, that the judgement theorist has overlooked the fact that an emotional response involves being pained or pleased by the situation. It is not clear, though, that this objection can be pressed home. The problem is that evaluative judgements are themselves often accompanied by feelings of pleasure or pain: judging that someone has let you down, for example, you may well feel pained by the thought. Hence, even if it is right to say that emotional responses involve feelings of pain and pleasure at the situation, the judgement theorist might still insist that it is a judgement that *occasions* the pain or pleasure; in other words, it is a judgement that initiates the response.

It is not clear, then, that the links between the phenomenal and intentional properties of emotion will provide us with a decisive objection to the judgement view. It is plausible that an emotional experience might itself constitute an evaluation of the situation. It is plausible, too, that emotional responses involve being pleased or pained by the situation. And if so, it will certainly be right to say that emotional responses involve intentional states that have a rich phenomenal character. Both these possibilities, though, are consistent with the claim that the evaluations that initiate emotional responses are evaluative judgements.

Recalcitrant Emotion

There is a second objection that is standardly brought against the judgement view. This, I shall suggest, does raise a serious problem for the judgement theorist.

Our emotional responses do not always reflect our judgements: in fact, they can sometimes conflict with them. Cases of this kind are known as cases of *recalcitrant emotion*. One striking example can be found in the literature on the psychology of disgust (Rozin et al., 1986). Paul Rozin and his colleagues conducted a series of experiments designed to test people's disgust reactions. They found that most of their subjects refused to drink apple juice that had been touched by a cockroach, even though they knew that the cockroach had been sterilized. Similarly, most subjects refused to eat fudge moulded to look like dog faeces, even though they knew that it was just fudge. They were disgusted by the thought of drinking or eating these things. Still, they seemed to realize that the apple juice had not been contaminated; they accepted too that the fudge was just fudge. Indeed, many of them were embarrassed by their emotional response (Rozin et al., 1986: 710).

Cases of recalcitrant emotion are common enough. I find the experience of riding a rollercoaster quite terrifying. But I do not judge that rollercoasters are dangerous: if I did, I would not allow my children to talk me into rollercoaster rides, let alone allow them to come too.[3] Again, someone might feel resentful about the extra time and attention that their parents gave to their chronically ill sibling, even though they accept that this was the right thing to do. A lifelong socialist might catch themselves feeling awed in the presence of wealthy and powerful people, despite believing that these people have merely profited from an unjust system.

Recalcitrant emotional responses need to be distinguished from another, rather different phenomenon. These are cases in which the subject has had a change of heart, but continues to feel worked up for a little while. In these cases, certain aspects of the subject's emotional experience (their bodily feelings, say) briefly persist, even though their evaluation$_i$ of the situation has changed. In cases of recalcitrant emotion, in contrast, the conflict persists long after the subject has had a chance to calm down; nor can it be resolved by taking a deep breath and counting to ten. This is significant, because it strongly suggests that emotional recalcitrance involves not only the feelings that emerge from the subject's emotional response, but also the evaluation$_i$ that initiates it. Emotional recalcitrance is, at root, a conflict between the subject's judgement and their emotional evaluation$_i$. This is why the phenomenon of emotional recalcitrance bears directly on the question that interests me here – the nature of emotional evaluations$_i$. We cannot understand how this kind of conflict can arise without understanding what these evaluations$_i$ are.

How might a judgement theorist account for cases of emotional recalcitrance? It looks as if they must insist that these are cases in which the subject has made two contradictory judgements. They must suppose, for example, that Rozin's subjects judge both that the juice is contaminated and that it is not contaminated. Admittedly, people do sometimes make contradictory judgements. I often catch myself with contradictory beliefs about my diary commitments: I believe I have a meeting after lunch, but then plan to do some writing that same afternoon. This situation, though, is not quite the same as the one that Rozin et al. describe. Once I notice the clash,

I take steps to resolve the contradiction: I check my diary; or I suspend judgement until I can find it. I do not go on believing that I am both free to do some writing and committed to a meeting at the same time.

Still, as Nussbaum points out, some beliefs are difficult to shake: as a child, she says, she came to believe that the US Supreme Court is in California; even though she now knows this is false, she still catches herself making this mistake (Nussbaum, 2001: 35–6). Presumably, though, Nussbaum is never consciously committed to these two contradictory judgements at the same time: when she remembers that the court is not in California, she stops thinking that it is – if only temporarily. Rozin's subjects, in contrast, seemed to accept that the juice is not contaminated, while feeling disgusted by it *at the same time*. Moreover, being told that the juice was safe to drink did not help them to overcome their disgust, even temporarily: it just made them feel embarrassed about their reaction. On the face of it, the conflict in this case does not look much like a conflict between two evaluative judgements.

In fact, we have already encountered this objection in a different guise in Chapter 2. As we saw there, there seems to be a difference between the following statements (Goldie, 2000: 74–6):

'Spiders are not really dangerous, but I am scared of them.'

'Spiders are not really dangerous, but I believe (or judge) that they are.'

The second statement strikes us as odd. There is something strange about a person endorsing one claim, while simultaneously admitting that they believe (or judge) something that obviously contradicts it. Unless they are very seriously confused, we would expect them to try to resolve the conflict. In contrast, the first statement does not seem particularly odd. As we have seen, people's emotional responses do sometimes conflict with their evaluative judgements; simply recognizing the conflict may not help to resolve it.

There is more to be said about the phenomenon of emotional recalcitrance. We will return to it, briefly, in the following section; and again, at rather more length, in Chapter 7. The point to note here is that this phenomenon raises a real difficulty for the judgement view. It looks very much as if emotional evaluations₁ are not directly responsive to reasoning in the way that judgements are – or at least, that this is not always the case. This constitutes a good reason to think that emotional evaluations₁ and evaluative judgements are different kinds of intentional state, produced by separate processes of evaluation.

same of
percep.

Emotional Evaluations₁ and Perceptions

Emotion and Perception Compared

In the previous section, we investigated the phenomenon of emotional recalcitrance. As I mentioned earlier, something similar can happen in the case of perceptual experience too: I see the spade handle as crooked, even though I know that it is straight. As many theorists of emotion have pointed out, these cases look very similar to cases of emotional recalcitrance: in particular, the subject's perception persists in the face of their judgement, just as the subject's emotional response persists in a case of emotional recalcitrance (Prinz, 2008: 157–8; Döring 2009; Tappolet, 2012). Similarly, as Sabine Döring points out (Döring, 2007: 379), there is nothing particularly odd about the following sentence:

> 'The spade handle is not really crooked, but I see it as crooked.'

This, then, seems to be a significant point of similarity between emotional evaluations₁ and perceptions: neither emotional evaluations₁ nor perceptions appear to be directly responsive to reasoning, in the way that judgements are.

It is possible to find some further parallels between emotion and perception. Consider the ways in which we are able to *control* our perceptual experiences. Even if we cannot just decide to perceive something in a particular way, we can exercise a measure of control over how things look or sound to us. We can do this, for example, by focusing our attention on a different set of perceptual cues, by drawing back to take a wider view, or just by looking at something from a different angle. In the longer term, it is possible to *educate* our perceptual sensibilities: someone might learn to attend to certain flavours in a particular dish; they might become better at hearing the harmonies in a complex piece of music. This is not a matter of rational persuasion or deliberation, but rather one of experience and practice.

Something similar seems to be true of our emotional evaluations$_i$. Suppose, for example, that you want to help a friend to overcome a tendency to react angrily to negative feedback on her work. It seems unlikely that you could do this through reasoned argument: after all, your friend may already know that her angry reactions are unreasonable. But you might well try to change how she *experiences* negative feedback: you might, for example, encourage her to view the situation in a different light ('Try to see it as coaching, not criticism') or remind her to pay attention to positive comments as well as negative ones. Doing this might her help her to cope better with feedback on a particular occasion. In the longer term, it might help to change her emotional sensibilities too. Again, though, this is a matter of experience and practice, rather than rational persuasion.

What about the phenomenal character of emotional evaluations$_i$? Can this be compared to perceptual phenomenology? This is a much harder question to answer, not least because there are several different claims that might be made. First, it might be suggested that emotional evaluations$_i$ are like perceptions, and unlike judgements, simply in *having* a phenomenal character. Earlier, I suggested that emotional evaluations$_i$ may indeed have phenomenal properties: an angry evaluation$_i$, perhaps, feels aggrieved and vengeful. If so, this is certainly a similarity between emotional evaluations$_i$ and perceptions. What is less clear, though, is whether this constitutes a contrast between an emotional evaluation$_i$ and a judgement: this will depend on whether judgements have a phenomenal character of some kind. As I mentioned earlier, this is a controversial issue.

Secondly, it might be suggested that emotional evaluations$_i$ are like perceptions, and unlike judgements, in that each type of evaluation₁ has a *specific* phenomenal character. The suggestion will be that an angry evaluation₁ feels different from a fearful evaluation₁, just as seeing an aubergine as purple feels different from tasting a mango as sweet. Certainly, anger and fear seem to involve different *urges*: in this respect, at least, an angry evaluation₁ might be thought to have a distinctive phenomenal character. However, not all types of emotional response involve an urge to act. In these cases, the question will turn on the quality of the pleasure or the pain involved. Does the pain of sorrow, for example, feel different to the pain of envy?[4] I find this hard to decide. Certainly, a sad response feels different from an envious response. But there are other considerations (bodily feelings, for example) that might explain the difference. Moreover, the seamless character of emotional experience, which I mentioned in Chapter 4, makes it hard to pin down exactly what explains the phenomenal character of a particular type of emotional response. I shall leave this as an open question.

Finally, it might be claimed that the phenomenal character of emotional evaluations₁ is *itself* perceptual in character. One reason someone might have for thinking this is that they hold that emotional evaluations₁ are themselves properly thought of as perceptions. I shall explore this suggestion in what follows.

Strong and Weak Perception Views

In the previous section, I described several ways in which emotional evaluations₁ appear to be similar to perceptual experiences. As I mentioned earlier, some theorists stop there: they hold that emotional evaluations₁ are like perceptions in a number of important ways, but they are not literally perceptions; rather they constitute a distinct class of intentional state. In what follows, I shall call this 'the weak perception view'. Other theorists go further: they argue that emotional evaluations₁ *are* perceptual experiences of some kind. I shall call this 'the strong perception view'. I have already offered some reasons to endorse a weak perception view. In what follows, I would like to consider the stronger claim.

There are at least three ways in which this stronger claim might be understood:

- Emotional evaluations$_i$ are bodily feelings.
- Emotional evaluations$_i$ are external sense perceptions.
- Emotional evaluations$_i$ constitute a distinct class of perceptions in their own right.

I shall begin by examining a version with which we are already familiar: the claim that emotional evaluations$_i$ are bodily feelings.

Emotional Evaluations$_i$ as Embodied Appraisals

Might emotional evaluations$_i$ be bodily feelings? We might recall Solomon's claim that bodily feelings can constitute 'judgements of the body'; or Prinz's claim that bodily feelings constitute an embodied appraisal of the situation. Both Solomon and Prinz hold that, in emotion, the subject's bodily feelings can signal that something emotionally significant is going on. Still, it is not altogether clear whether we should think of these states as emotional evaluations$_i$. The reason is one we met earlier, when we considered Montague's argument: the subject's bodily feelings do not *initiate* the emotional response; rather, they are generated by it.

In the case of Prinz's account, however, the issue is not clear-cut. The reason lies with Prinz's account of the structure of an emotional response. As we saw in Chapter 2, Prinz holds that the bodily changes happen first, while other changes – in particular, changes to motivation – occur only later, in response to the subject's embodied appraisal and its accompanying valence marker. There is certainly room to question whether Prinz is right about this. Suppose, though, that we grant Prinz this empirical claim. If so, we could at least say that embodied appraisals have the job of initiating an important *part* of an emotional response – the psychological changes that occur after the bodily changes are underway. If so, Prinz's account might be classified as a version of the strong perception view.

Once we have conceded all this, though, it should be clear that embodied appraisals cannot be the *only* intentional states involved in initiating an emotional response. Something must have happened earlier – a perception or a judgement – to prompt the bodily changes on which the embodied appraisal depends. This earlier representation must have identified the situation as an emotionally significant one – as dangerous, for example; if not, it is hard to see why it should trigger the bodily changes appropriate to fear.

Moreover, on Prinz's account, the content of an embodied appraisal is very thin. In a case of fear, for example, the embodied appraisal means something like 'Danger here now!', while the valence marker means something like 'This is bad!'. These two signals carry no information about the source of the threat. Hence, they cannot by themselves explain why the subject's attention switches to the source of the danger or why it is *that* object or situation they are motivated to flee.[5] To explain this, Prinz suggests, we need to appeal to further representations – beliefs or perceptions – which locate the source of the danger. These further representations will play a crucial role in explaining how the subject's emotional response develops.

Putting these two considerations together, we might worry that, on Prinz's account, the combination of embodied appraisal and valence marker has very little *work* to do: it is neither the intentional state that first registers the presence of a threat, nor is it the intentional state that identifies the source of the threat. It is, at best, one of a number of evaluations that help to shape the emotional response.

Sense Perceptions and Affective Perceptions

In this section, I shall consider two other versions of the strong perception view: the view that emotional evaluations are external sense perceptions and the view that they constitute a class of perceptions in their own right.

I shall start with the first of these: the idea will be that Bill literally *sees* Monty as dangerous; Alice literally *hears* the slamming door as an assault. This suggestion, however, faces an immediate and strong objection. To say that I see or hear something implies that I am in a particular kind of causal contact with it. To say that I can hear my neighbours quarrelling in their garden, for example, implies that sound waves generated by their quarrel are reaching my eardrums. In contrast, I can become angry or happy about something that happened many years ago; or about something that might happen in the future. I do not have to see or hear these things for myself: it is enough that I remember or imagine them. This looks like a decisive objection to the claim that emotional evaluations$_i$ just *are* sense perceptions of external objects.

An alternative approach is to claim that emotional evaluations$_i$ are neither bodily feelings nor sense perceptions, but rather constitute a third class of perceptions.[6] Döring (2003, 2007), for example, suggests that we should classify emotional evaluations$_i$ as 'affective perceptions' (see also Tappolet, 2012). This is justified, she thinks, by the similarities between emotional evaluations$_i$ and sense perceptions. These are strong enough, she argues, to warrant taking these states to belong to the same broad psychological category. Given the similarities that we have found between emotional evaluations$_i$ and perceptions, it might well be thought that this view has some plausibility. Nevertheless, I want to end by mentioning two objections that might be brought to it – and indeed to any version of the strong perception view. I shall describe these difficulties only briefly here; I shall discuss them in detail in Chapter 7.

Evaluations$_i$, Reasons and Grounds

Earlier, I suggested that there are several ways in which emotional evaluations$_i$ can be compared to perceptions. This leaves it open, however, that there are also some significant ways in which emotional evaluations$_i$ *differ* from perceptual experiences. Finding these contrasts would not refute the weak perception view. However, it would pose a challenge to the stronger claim that emotional evaluations$_i$ literally *are* perceptions of some kind. At the very least, the strong perception theorist would need to find a way to explain these contrasts without undermining the claim that emotional evaluations; are perceptions. Moreover, there appear to be at least two possible candidates for this role.

(1) *Recalcitrance again.* Earlier, I argued that cases of recalcitrant emotion raise a problem for judgement theories. However, as Helm has pointed out (Helm, 2001: 41–6), they pose a challenge for perception theorists too. The problem is that recalcitrant emotions are often described as *irrational*. Many of Rozin's subjects, for example, described their disgust in this way (Rozin et al., 1986: 710). In contrast, perceptual experiences that conflict with the subject's beliefs are not described as irrational: as we saw earlier, it is not irrational to see a spade handle as crooked, even when you know that it is straight.

(2) *Reasons for emotion.* As we have seen, our perceptual experiences are not based on reasons: when I see an aubergine as purple, this is not because I have a reason to see it as purple: it just strikes me that way. In contrast, if I *judge* that it is purple, I may well have a reason for doing so – for example, the fact that it looks purple. I can appeal to my reason to explain and justify my belief. Similarly, people do often talk as if they have reasons or grounds for their emotional responses. Bill, for example, might claim that he has good grounds to fear Monty: pythons, after all, have been known to kill people, and Monty, perhaps, is a very large python. The claim that Bill has good grounds to fear Monty does not seem to be equivalent to the claim that Bill's fear fits the situation. Even if Monty turns out to be perfectly harmless, Bill might still claim to have had good grounds for fear (cf. Brady, 2007: 275–6).

In both these respects, then, emotional evaluations; might be thought to differ from perceptual experiences. Admittedly, it is not obvious that we should take these ways of talking about emotion at face value. Certainly, it is not immediately obvious how they can be reconciled with some of the claims about emotional evaluations; that I have made in this chapter – in particular, the claim that they are not directly responsive to reasoning. Indeed, one possible explanation is that we talk in these ways because we are in the grip of a theory: we are mistakenly thinking of emotional evaluations; as judgements or beliefs. Now, if we already had very strong reasons to think that emotional evaluations; literally are perceptions, this would be a convincing response. What we have established, so far, though, is not that emotional evaluations₁ are perceptions, but only that they are like perceptions in some significant respects. This is not a reason to insist they are like perceptions in every respect.

On the face of, then, it does look as if we should take seriously these ways of talking about emotion. This is not to say, of course, that we should now jump the other way and return to the judgement view. It may yet turn out that, on closer examination, these phenomena can be accommodated by some version of the strong perception view. Alternatively, a weak perception theorist can allow that emotional evaluations₁ have *some* features in common with judgements. In Chapter 7, I shall investigate this issue.

Summary

I have argued that there are good reasons to deny that emotional evaluations₁ are judgements. In particular, the phenomenon of recalcitrant emotion suggests that emotional evaluations₁ and judgements are produced by different processes of evaluation. Indeed, there seem to be some respects in which emotional evaluations₁ are similar to perceptions, rather than judgements. This raises the possibility that we might take a step further, and adopt a strong perception view. As we have seen, there are several ways in which this kind of account might be developed. I have argued that emotional evaluations₁ are not best thought of as bodily feelings or external sense perceptions, but I have not offered any decisive argument against Döring's view that they are affective perceptions. I ended, however, by flagging up two apparent contrasts between emotion and perception. I shall return to these in Chapter 7.

Further Reading

Theorists who hold that emotional evaluations₁ are, or involve, judgements or beliefs include Lyons (1980); Marks

(1982); Shaffer (1983); Nash (1989); Solomon (1993 [1976]: Chap. 5; 2003a [1988]); Nussbaum (2001: Chap. 1). Proponents of the strong perception theory include Döring (2003, 2007); Prinz (2004: Chaps 3 and 10); Deonna (2006); Tappolet (2012). For some views sympathetic to the weak perception theory, see de Sousa (1987: Chap. 6); Goldie (2000: Chap. 3); Brady (2009); Montague (2009). For a view of emotional evaluations; as 'concerned construals', see Roberts (1988); and as 'felt evaluations', see Helm (2009). If you wish to explore the debate about the phenomenal character of beliefs and judgements, you might want to investigate the discussions in Bayne and Montague (2011), especially the very helpful introduction.

5
What Are Emotional Evaluations About?

Introduction

In this chapter, I shall investigate the intentional properties of emotion – and, in particular, of emotional evaluations$_i$. What do our emotional evaluations$_i$ tell us? Or to put it another way, under what circumstances does an emotional evaluation$_i$ *fit* the situation?

My discussion will fall into two parts. In the following section, I shall focus on a particular emotional evaluation$_i$ – Bill's fearful evaluation$_i$ of Monty. I shall investigate how the content of this evaluation$_i$ reflects the particular structure and function of the fearful response that it prompts. In doing this, I shall highlight some ways in which the content of Bill's evaluation$_i$ might be thought to differ from the content of the evaluative judgement that Monty is dangerous. I shall draw some contrasts, too, with other types of emotional evaluation$_i$. Indeed, I have chosen to focus on Bill's fearful evaluation$_i$ because this example is particularly suited to drawing out these contrasts.

In the third section, I shall investigate a specific question about the content of emotional evaluations$_i$. As we saw in Chapter 2, Solomon suggests that emotions have a 'self-involved' quality: to respond emotionally to a situation, he suggests, involves taking the situation to have a particular kind of significance for *oneself*. But what kind of significance is this? As we shall see, this is not an easy question to answer. Nevertheless, the question is worth spending some time on: as I shall explain, answering this question can help us to better understand the importance of emotion in our personal lives.

How might we set about answering these questions? One strategy is to approach them via a particular theory of intentional content. Appealing to a theory of content should allow us to develop a coherent and principled account, which has the support of a more general theory. Nevertheless, this approach has its difficulties. For one thing, there are many different theories of content to choose from, and no shortage of debate about their relative merits. Moreover, there is no guarantee that this strategy will yield a decisive answer to every question we might ask: this is because what the theory implies in any particular case will depend, in part, on the facts of that case, and in some cases we may not know what these are.

Alternatively, we might appeal to our intuitions about particular cases. This approach will be reliable insofar as our intuitions accurately reflect the intentional properties that our emotional evaluations actually have. However, there is no guarantee that this is so in every case: our intuitions might sometimes reflect mistaken assumptions about the nature of emotion. Still, this approach might at least help us to decide which account is the most *plausible*, even if this is unlikely to settle the issue decisively. Both these approaches, then, have their limitations. In what follows, I shall rely on the first as far as I can, but I shall need to make some appeals to intuition too.

This is not the place to discuss the merits of different theories of content. Instead, I shall begin by helping myself to a particular theory – one I have developed and defended elsewhere (Price, 2001). It is a kind of *teleosemantic* theory. Teleosemanticists hold that the content of an intentional state is determined by its functional properties. Hence, in making use of this theory, I shall again be taking the functional approach to emotion introduced in Chapter 3. Indeed in this chapter, functional considerations will take centre stage.

My first task is to set out this theory of content. I shall begin with a little scene-setting: my aim is just to provide some sense of the way in which teleosemanticists view intentional content, and why they are attracted by this kind of account. Having introduced the theory, I shall explain how we might use it to characterize the content of Bill's fearful evaluation$_i$.

Function, Content and the Case of Fear

Why Teleosemantics?

Teleosemantic theories of content have been developed by a number of theorists, including Ruth Millikan (1984), Fred Dretske (1995) and Karen Neander (1995). Although they differ on details, all these theorists agree that the content of an intentional state depends on the causal role that it is supposed to play in our psychology. They agree too that the phrase 'is supposed to' is to be understood in functional terms: it concerns what the state functions to do or what it normally does. Moreover, most teleosemantic theorists assume a historical theory of functions of the kind that I set out in Chapter 3: on this kind of theory, to say that an item has a certain function, or that it is performing its function in a normal way, is to make a claim about its causal history.

According to teleosemantic theories, then, facts about intentional content are, ultimately, facts about the causal properties of intentional states. Theories that account for intentional content in causal terms are sometimes labelled 'naturalistic' theories of content. One attractive feature of these accounts is that they allow us to understand intentional content as an instance of a phenomenon that is already familiar and pervasive. After all, we commonly describe and classify things in terms of their causal properties. (A very simple example is a signature: to describe something as my signature implies that I am its cause.) Naturalistic accounts imply that talk of intentionality is just another instance of this everyday phenomenon. Moreover, on this kind of account, it is relatively easy to understand how we can appeal to people's intentional states (their beliefs and desires, say) to explain their behaviour: intentional explanations will turn out to be causal explanations of some kind. Finally, some theorists who endorse naturalism do so, in part, because they are looking for a notion of intentional content that could be used within a scientific theory of the mind: a central concern of science is to understand the causal structure of the world.

Teleosemantic theories differ from other naturalistic accounts in one crucial respect: they are concerned not with the causal role that intentional states *in fact* play, but rather with the role that they *normally* play. Teleosemanticists often claim that this gives their approach an advantage over other naturalistic accounts. This is because it makes it particularly easy to accommodate the fact that intentional states can *mis*represent the situation – that beliefs can be false or perceptions inaccurate. Suppose, for example, that, gazing out of a train window, I see (what appears to be) a hippopotamus standing in a pond. On a teleosemantic theory, to say that my visual experience represents its object as a hippopotamus is to imply that it is *normally* produced in response to a hippopotamus. But 'normally' does not mean 'always'; it does not even mean 'typically' or 'often'. Hence, this view leaves plenty of room for the possibility that my visual experience is mistaken.

As I said earlier, all these claims are open to dispute. It is controversial whether naturalistic theories can fully account for intentionality; it is controversial, too, whether teleosemantic theories cope with misrepresentation as smoothly as I have suggested; or whether they run into difficulties of other kinds.[1] As I have been emphasizing, though, my aim is not to defend this approach, but to put it to use in developing an account of emotional evaluations$_i$. If the teleosemantic theory fails, we will need to think again. Even so, it is possible that some of the considerations I highlight here would be important on other theories of content too.

Some Basic Concepts

My next task is to set out the teleosemantic theory that I am going to assume. Teleosemantic theories have an unfortunate tendency to become very convoluted. In what follows, I shall present only the essentials, and I shall proceed in small steps. I shall start by presenting some basic concepts and claims.

(1) *Functions.* If emotional evaluations$_i$ have functions, what kind of functions do they have? As I mentioned in Chapter 3, I am assuming that the systems that produce emotional evaluations$_i$ are *biological* systems: they are neurophysiological mechanisms in the brain, shaped by natural selection. It may help, then, to recall the account of biological functions that I presented in Chapter 3. To say that a biological organ (my liver, say) has a certain function (storing vitamin A, say) implies the following:

- My ancestors possessed similar organs that stored vitamin A.
- Those organs achieved this by themselves, and not in concert with other organs or systems.
- By doing this they directly contributed to the workings of other organs and systems in my ancestors' bodies.
- All this helps to explain why my liver exists today.

My liver will be performing this function *normally* if it is storing vitamin A in just the way that these earlier organs did.

(2) *Intentional systems.* Intentional states are produced by intentional *systems*. These range from the simple signalling system that prompts you to blink when something approaches your eye to the highly sophisticated systems that generate your beliefs and desires. Intentional systems are *control* systems: they function to control the behaviour of some other, dependent mechanism or system. By doing this, they help this second, dependent system to behave in a way that is appropriate, given the situation – for example, by prompting it to respond at the right time (Millikan, 1984: 96–102; Price, 2001: 75–8). They do this by exploiting *information* (e.g. perceptual information) about the environment (Price, 2001: 90–3). As an example, consider the signalling system that controls blinking. This system functions to ensure that the relevant muscles produce a blink when a blink is needed; it normally does this by triggering a blink in response to the information that something is approaching the eye.

Earlier, I described intentional systems as biological systems, shaped by natural selection. In describing them in these terms, I do not mean to imply that their workings are determined wholly by their evolutionary history. In many cases, the way in which an intentional system normally works can be modified by learning. Through learning, an intentional system might come to exploit new sources of information or control different kinds of behaviour. Exactly how this occurs depends on the functions of the mechanisms that control the process of learning and on the way in which those mechanisms normally work (Price, 2001: 125–36). The point to note here, though, is simply that the capacity to learn is itself a normal feature of many intentional systems.

(3) *Descriptive and directive content.* In Chapter 5, I distinguished between two classes of intentional state. Beliefs and perceptions, I suggested, represent how things actually are, while desires represent goals to be achieved or activities to be performed. We might say that beliefs and perceptions have *descriptive* content, while desires have *directive* content. Arguably, some intentional states possess a combination of descriptive and directive content (Millikan, 1995). It might be thought that pain is a state of this kind: it signals that the subject has been hurt, but it also motivates particular kinds of behaviour. I am going to suggest that a fearful evaluation$_i$ possesses a combination of descriptive and directive content (de Sousa, 1987: 120–1; Price, 2006a: 217).

Bill's Fearful Evaluation$_i$: An Initial Sketch

We are now in a position to consider how we might determine the intentional content of Bill's fearful evaluation$_i$. In this section, I shall offer a rough sketch; in the next section, I shall fill in some further details.

Consider, first, the evaluative system that produces Bill's evaluation$_i$. This is an intentional system: its job is to control the various psychological, physiological and behavioural mechanisms that help to generate his fearful response. The evaluative system controls these mechanisms by producing fearful evaluations$_i$ in response to information about the situation: in this way, it helps to ensure that Bill's fearful responses perform their function effectively. I want to suggest that it does this in two ways.

One function of the evaluative system is to ensure that Bill produces a fearful response at the right time – that is, when the situation calls for fear. This is what makes it right to say that Bill's fearful evaluation$_i$ has descriptive content of some kind. But what kind? According to the teleosemantic theory that I am assuming here, this will depend on the answers to two questions (Price, 2001:104):

- What conditions normally need to be in place if a fearful response is to perform its function effectively?
- What conditions is the evaluative system normally *able* to detect? In other words, what information is it normally sensitive to?

There are several conditions that need to be in place if a fearful response is to perform its function in the normal way. Most obviously, Bill must be facing a serious physical threat. We might bear in mind, too, that a fearful response will not normally be of much use if Bill is completely immobilized, or if the response would only make things worse – for example, by triggering a fatal heart attack. Unfortunately, Bill's evaluative system is not normally able to detect whether he is immobilized or whether he is on the brink of a heart attack. We cannot say, then, that it functions to detect these things. However, the system *is* normally able to detect that Bill is facing a serious physical threat. By doing this, it helps to ensure that his fearful responses succeed in performing their function. This is why it is right to say that Bill's fearful evaluation$_i$ signals that he is facing such a threat.

The evaluative system has a second task to perform: it prompts Bill to try to resolve the situation – in this case, by fleeing into his house. Bill's fearful behaviour has a particular function – to ensure that he avoids injury. Nevertheless, it is not a pre-programmed reflex response, like a blink. Rather, it takes account of the particular features of the situation – the speed of Monty's approach, the location of his house, and so on. For this to be possible, Bill must (however hurriedly) *choose* a course of action – one that is tailored to the situation. Bill's fearful evaluation$_i$ helps to ensure that he makes a good choice. It does this by *motivating* him to try to avoid injury. In other words, it ensures that, when he chooses what to do, he is aiming at the right goal. This is why it is right to say that Bill's evaluation$_i$ has directive, as well as descriptive, content: it represents avoiding injury as a goal to be achieved (Price, 2001: 136–41; 2006a: 217–18).

Filling in the Details

As a first stab, then, it looks as if the content of Bill's fearful evaluation$_i$ might be expressed (very roughly) as follows:

> F1   'This situation poses a serious physical threat! Take steps to avoid injury now!'

This, though, is not the end of the story: a fearful response has other features that we have yet to consider. In this section, I shall fill in some further details. Doing this will involve taking account of the particular structure and function of the fearful response that Bill's evaluation$_i$ is supposed to prompt.

(1) *Identifying the source.* As I emphasized in Chapter 5, Bill's fearful response is not just a reaction to the presence of a threat: it is directed specifically at *Monty*. In particular, Bill's attention is directed onto Monty; and it is Monty that Bill is motivated to flee. Moreover, Bill's fearful evaluation$_i$ is normally able to ensure that his fearful response is directed at the right target: this is because it normally carries the information not just that Bill is facing a threat, but that Monty is the *source* of the threat; and it motivates Bill not just to avoid injury, but to avoid being injured *by Monty*. Hence, its content should look more like this:

> F2   'That snake poses a serious physical threat! Take steps to avoid being injured by it now!'

(2) *Complex directive content.* The directive content of Bill's evaluation$_i$ may be more complex than F1 implies. It has been suggested (Tooby and Cosmides, 1990) that one function of a fearful response is to speed up decision-making,

by limiting the behavioural options that the subject is likely to consider. The suggestion will be that Bill's evaluation$_i$ does not motivate him just to try to avoid being injured, but also to do this in one of a limited number of ways – by fleeing, lashing out or hiding, say. This suggestion has some plausibility. Imagine that Bill knows that the best way to avoid being injured by a snake is not to flee, but to discourage it by spraying it gently with a hose. Still, given how frightened Bill is on this occasion, it would not be surprising if this course of action never occurs to him; and if it does, he might find it very hard to bring himself to do it. Indeed, it would seem rather odd to say that Bill gently hosed Monty *out of fear*: we might be more inclined to say that he did this *despite* his fear. In contrast, it is not strange to say that Bill fled Monty or lashed out at him or hid from him out of fear. This suggests that we might make a further adjustment to F1:

F3   'That snake poses a serious physical threat! Take steps to avoid being injured, by fleeing from it, lashing out at it or hiding from it now!'

In this respect, Bill's evaluation$_i$ seems to differ from the evaluative belief 'That snake is dangerous'. This belief might well incline Bill to try to keep away from the snake, to warn others, and so on. But it need not incline him to do these things in any particular way: that will depend on his other beliefs and desires. Indeed, this seems to be a point of contrast with other types of emotional evaluation$_i$, too. Anxiety prompts the subject to look for a way to resolve the situation; but it does not seem to motivate them to adopt a particular *kind* of solution. One reason may be that anxiety is not concerned with a specific type of threat – one can be anxious about many different kinds of thing. Moreover, anxiety is not an emergency response: it can be directed at threats that are still some distance away, giving the subject more time to decide what to do. Because fear and anxiety have different functions, fearful and anxious evaluations$_i$ may well be structured in different ways (Price 2006a: 218, 220–1).

(3) *Temporal content.* Bill's fearful evaluation$_i$ has a specific temporal content: it concerns a threat that he is facing *now*; and it motivates him to act *now*. Other types of

emotional evaluation; have different kinds of temporal content: regret and remorse are concerned with past events; while anxiety and hope concern events that may happen in the future. As Philip Percival (1992) has pointed out, this is a further contrast between emotion and belief. Beliefs are not tied to a particular timeframe: I might believe that something is dangerous now; but I can also believe that it was dangerous in the past, or that it will be dangerous in the future. Moreover, this difference can once again be explained in functional terms. The function of Bill's fearful evaluation; is to ensure that he takes immediate steps to defuse a threat that confronts him now. If Monty has long since died of old age, there is no point in Bill continuing to fear him. But there is still some point in his continuing to believe that Monty was dangerous: this belief might usefully influence his behaviour in many different ways (Price, 2006a: 218, 223–5).

(4) *Degree of threat.* A further function of Bill's evaluation; is to ensure that the intensity of his fearful response is *proportional* to the situation. To do this, it needs to include an assessment of the seriousness of the threat. This assessment might well reflect a range of factors: the probability that Bill will be injured; the severity of the injury; its closeness in time. There is no reason to assume that Bill's evaluation; represents each of these factors separately: it would need to do this only if each factor normally affects Bill's response in a different way. Assuming this is not the case, what constitutes a serious threat might turn out to be something rather idiosyncratic. In particular, there is no reason to assume that it correlates to some concept 'degree of danger' that features in Bill's evaluative beliefs: 'very frightening' and 'very dangerous' might well turn out to be rather different things (Price, 2006a: 225–6).

I have suggested that Bill's evaluation; has a rather complex content, reflecting the complexity of the response that it functions to prompt. Moreover, because it has a rather specialized function – to prompt a particular kind of emotional response – its content may well be rather specialized too. This seems to be true of the temporal content of a fearful evaluation;; and it may also be true of the way in which a fearful evaluation; represents the seriousness of the threat. It may turn out, then, that the content of Bill's evaluation; is not exactly equivalent to the content of the evaluative judgement that Monty is dangerous – even if it implies that this judgement is correct.

The Problem of Emotional Significance

What Is the Problem?

In the previous section, I offered an account of the content of Bill's fearful evaluation$_i$. As it stands, this account leaves an important question unresolved.

Bill's fearful evaluation$_i$, I suggested, represents Monty as posing a serious physical threat. It does not seem too hard to say what this means: it implies that there is a real possibility that Monty will inflict serious injury or pain on Bill. When we consider other types of emotion, however, matters are not so simple. Consider, for example, a sad evaluation$_i$. Sadness is normally elicited by a *loss* of some kind. But not every loss is a proper object of sadness: the loss of a headache, for example, is not usually a sad loss. Sadness is concerned only with losses that have a particular kind of significance. The same can be said about other emotions too: joy is concerned with significant successes, anxiety with significant setbacks, and so on. But what *counts* as a significant success? What counts as a significant setback?

The answer is far from obvious.[2] Still, without an answer to this question, we cannot spell out the conditions under which our emotional responses fit the situation. Moreover, the question bears on some broader issues about the value of emotions and the role that they play in our practical lives. Consider a case in which your emotional response is out of step with your considered judgement. Might you have reason to reconsider your judgement in the light of your emotional response? Or should you simply dismiss your response as a 'gut reaction', with no power to challenge your judgements? The answer depends, in part, on what our emotional evaluations$_i$ are *about*: do they indicate something *important* about the situation – something that you care about or have reason to care about? I shall return to this issue in Chapter 7.

Emotional Significance as Personal Significance

We have already come across an account of emotional significance. As I mentioned in Chapter 2, Robert Solomon suggests that to respond emotionally to a situation involves taking it to have a particular kind of *personal* significance. Indeed, many theorists have made similar suggestions. Aaron Ben-Ze'ev (2000: 18), for example, suggests that emotional responses relate to the subject's personal preferences; Jesse Prinz (2004: 63) suggests that a sad loss is the loss of something that one *values*; while Martha Nussbaum (2001: 30–3) suggests that emotions are concerned with the subject's *flourishing*. It looks, then, as if these theorists agree on something like the following claim:

> P   Emotionally significant situations are ones that bear on the subject's personal concerns.[3]

Is P correct? Certainly, it does not seem to apply in every case. As I mentioned in Chapter 1, we can distinguish between different classes of emotion: for example, we might distinguish moral emotions (indignation or remorse, say) from personal emotions (anxiety, sadness, etc.). P does not seem to be true of moral emotional responses. Suppose that I am remorseful about something – breaking a promise, say. Plausibly, to claim that my behaviour merits remorse is to make a *moral* claim: it implies that I was responsible for my action and that it was morally wrong. How my action impacted on my personal concerns – whether I was harmed by breaking my promise or whether I care about breaking it – seems to be beside the point.

On the other hand, if we focus on personal emotional responses, P seems much more plausible. Suppose that I am *sad* about something I have done: dropping a teacup, say. Plausibly, whether I am right to feel sad rests on how the situation impacts on *me*: will the loss of the cup leave me worse off in some sense? If this is right, we can at least say that P is true of a large and important class of emotional responses: these might include cases of sorrow, joy, anxiety, love, hate, jealousy, envy, grief, fear, disgust, embarrassment, gratitude, relief, regret, dread and hope, as well as some cases of anger, shame and pride. In what follows, I am going to focus on responses of these kinds.

The next thing to note is that P is open to more than one interpretation, depending on what we take the subject's concerns to be. Ben-Ze'ev and Prinz both focus on the subject's *preferences*: they take personal significance to be a matter of what the subject values, wants or cares about. Nussbaum, in contrast, identifies the subject's concerns with their *flourishing* – the satisfaction of their needs or interests. It looks, then, as if there is room for at least two different kinds of account: one that focuses on the subject's preferences and one that focuses on their interests. We might wonder, then, which approach we would do best to adopt.

In what follows, I want to explore this issue further. I shall start by looking more carefully at some of the concepts that I have introduced in this section. What interests do people have? What constitutes a preference? How do our interests and our preferences connect?

Interests and Preferences

Interests

We might identify a person's interests with the satisfaction of their preferences or the happiness that results. Here, though, I am casting the interest-based account as an *alternative* to a preference-based account; so I cannot define someone's interests in terms of their preferences. Instead, I shall assume an 'objective list' theory of interests (Parfit, 1984: 499; Scanlon, 1998). According to this kind of theory, certain goods are required for a successful human life, regardless of whether we want or value them. These might include any or all of the following:

- health;
- security;
- adequate material resources;
- good social status;
- autonomy;
- good social relationships;
- intellectual stimulation.

What is in a person's interests, on this view, is to possess goods of these kinds.

How should we decide what to include on the list? One possibility is that we should understand claims about interests as *evaluative* claims – as claims about the kind of life that people *ought to* have. Nussbaum might be ascribed a view of this kind: when she suggests that emotional responses are concerned with the subject's flourishing, she is appealing to an Aristotelian view of well-being that embodies a particular set of ethical values. (Hence, on her view, the distinction between personal and moral emotional responses is rather less clear-cut than I suggested earlier.) But there are other possible approaches. In particular, someone who wants to combine an interest-based account with a teleosemantic theory of content will naturally think of interests *historically* – as the resources that have helped human beings to survive and to produce healthy offspring. Because I am assuming a teleosemantic theory, this is the approach that I shall take here.

Preferences

Preferences come in various forms. Here, I shall distinguish three different kinds of preference.

- *Values.* I shall use this term to mean the subject's *established evaluative beliefs* about what, in general, it is worth respecting, promoting or pursuing.
- *Desires.* These are purely motivational states. Desires are not all of a kind: someone's considered desire to visit India is not quite the same kind of thing as an urge to yawn. Here, though, I shall treat them as a single category.
- *Likes and dislikes.* To like something (as I shall use the term here) is to have a settled disposition to experience it as pleasant or enjoyable; to dislike something is to have a settled disposition to experience it as unpleasant or distressing. Our likes and dislikes are manifested by a variety of feelings – physical pain or comfort, excitement, boredom, satisfaction, frustration, relief, disappointment, loneliness, elation, misery, and so on. They

range from mild proclivities and aversions to fervent loves and hates.

Our values, desires and likes are closely linked: in particular, our desires and our values often reflect our likes. But these states can conflict: I might want to go ice-skating, only to discover that I hate it; I might enjoy day-dreaming, while believing that day-dreaming is an unforgivable waste of time. In the first case, the conflict arises because I am *mistaken* about my likes: I imagine, incorrectly, that ice-skating is something that I would enjoy. In the second case, it arises because my values are grounded in something – a moral or personal ideal, perhaps – that is independent of my likes.

Connecting interests and preferences

People's preferences often reflect their interests: goods such as health, intellectual stimulation and social interaction are things that people tend to value, want and enjoy. There seems to be a particularly close connection between our likes and our interests: it is natural to regard feelings of physical comfort as signalling the satisfaction of basic bodily needs; while feelings of boredom or loneliness relate to our intellectual and social needs (Millgram, 1993: 401). In other cases, our likes reflect the particular *ways* we have found to satisfy our interests: I might come to enjoy amateur dramatics, for example, because I have learned that this is a way for me to make friends. In these cases, our likes reflect not just our shared biological needs, but also our experiences as individuals.

Still, it is important not to overstate the relationship between preferences and interests. For one thing, our preferences are not always an *accurate* guide to our interests: we make bad friendships and eat unhealthy food because our preferences fail to track our needs. Moreover, some of our preferences are quite independent of our interests. People can have moral or personal ideals – a commitment to environmental justice, say – that do nothing to further their interests. They can develop likes that are quite independent of their needs: a parachutist, for example, might simply enjoy the excitement of the jump. In what follows, I shall refer to these as *idle preferences*.

Contrasting Interest-Based and Preference-Based Accounts

We are now in a position to draw some contrasts between interest-based and preference-based accounts. On an interest-based account, personally significant successes might include improving your health or strengthening a valuable friendship; personally significant setbacks might include a drop in social status or being deprived of your freedom. This is not because you care about these things, but because, without them, you cannot normally thrive. Moreover, to the extent that human beings share the same interests, they should also find the same things personally significant: if losing your freedom is sad for you, losing my freedom should be sad for me too. On a preference-based account, in contrast, it is far harder to say what might count as a personally significant situation: this will depend on the subject's particular preferences. On a preference-based account, then, we cannot say that a situation is sad full stop: rather, it is sad *for you*, or sad *for me*, depending on our preferences.

An interest-based account implies that personal emotional responses are always concerned with the subject's *own* interests. Indeed, this might look like a difficulty for the account: on the face of it, we can fittingly feel sorrow, anxiety or joy for someone else. As I watch fire-fighters trying to rescue someone from a fire, for example, I might fittingly feel anxious or relieved, even if everyone involved is a stranger (Tappolet, 2010). In fact, the interest-based theorist need not deny this, but they do need to take extra steps to account for it: one solution might be to treat feelings for others as a separate class of emotional response, involving a different kind of emotional significance. In contrast, a preference-based theorist can easily accommodate the fact that we sometimes feel sorrow or anxiety for somebody else. This is because we can have preferences concerning other people. Someone might take pleasure in watching other people enjoy themselves; they might be distressed when they see someone else in pain.

Finally, there is an ambiguity that is worth quickly noting: do these accounts imply that the personal significance of the situation depends on how it affects my interests or preferences *overall*? Or does it depend on how it affects *at least one* of my interests or preferences? I shall not discuss this issue here, though I shall come back to it in Chapter 7.

Introducing the Likes-Based Account

The account that I favour is a particular kind of preference-based account: it is the view that the personal significance of a situation depends on the subject's likes and dislikes, their loves and hates. I shall refer to this as the *likes-based account*. On this account, a situation will have positive personal significance for the subject if it is one that they have a settled disposition to experience as pleasant; it will have negative personal significance if it is one that they have a settled disposition to experience as distressing.

In fact, I am not sure that this account can be applied in all cases involving a personal emotional response. Consider, for example, shame at one's lack of sporting prowess, or admiration for the achievements of a great explorer. On the face of it, these are personal emotional responses: certainly, they do not seem to be *moral* responses. Arguably, though, these responses relate to the subject's values, rather than their likes. Nevertheless, I do think that the likes-based approach works well for a large class of personal emotional responses. These include, for example, sorrow, anxiety and joy.

However, although I am attracted to the likes-based account, I am not in a position to present a decisive argument for it here. In particular (and for reasons that I shall explain later on), the issue cannot be resolved simply by appealing to the teleosemantic theory. My discussion here, then, will have rather limited aims: I want to establish, first, that this account is at least *consistent* with the teleosemantic theory; secondly, I shall argue that the account has some intuitive plausibility. My discussion, therefore, will have a somewhat tentative and exploratory feel. Nevertheless, I hope to establish that the account is at least worth taking seriously. I shall start, in what remains of this section, by defending the account against a couple of immediate objections.

One worry someone might have about this account is that it implies that our emotional responses are rather trivial: they will be trivial, it might be thought, because likes or dislikes are themselves trivial things – mere passing fancies. I hope, though, that I have already provided sufficient material to head off this objection. Our likes and dislikes, I have suggested, are fundamental concerns of ours. They include not only mild proclivities, but also our most fervent loves and hates. In many cases, they reflect our interests, as biological and social beings; but they are also shaped by our experience of the world. They are important and enduring aspects of our characters, and the source of many of our desires and values.

There is another, more subtle, objection that might be raised to the account. The objection starts from the thought that there is already a close relationship between likes and emotions: liking something is *itself* partly a matter of having certain emotional dispositions towards it – for example, liking something might involve finding it uplifting or cheering. Hence the likes-based account amounts to no more than the claim that an emotional response will be appropriate if the subject is inclined to have emotional responses of just that kind in this kind of situation. But if so (the objection continues), the likes-based account will have a very unfortunate implication: it will imply that an emotional evaluation; can never be misplaced. Suppose, for example, that I am filled with joy as I watch the sun set behind the mountains: the fact that I respond to the sunset with joy *entails* that I have a disposition to experience the situation as joyous; in other words, it entails that I like sunsets. Hence, my joyful reaction is *guaranteed* to fit the situation, according to the likes-based account.

I am happy to concede that, on the likes-based account, there are cases in which an emotional response fits the situation simply because the subject has a (settled) disposition to experience that emotion in that kind of situation. If a sunset fills me with joy, there may be very little I can say to explain why: it is just that sunsets are the sort of thing that makes me happy. Still, the likes-based account does not imply that my joy on this occasion cannot be misplaced. In fact, there are two different ways in which this can occur. First, I may be mistaken about what I am seeing: perhaps it is not a sunset at all, but the glow of a forest fire. Secondly, my joy may not manifest a *settled* disposition of mine. Perhaps I do not really like sunsets at all, but am briefly caught up in a sentimental fantasy about the glories of nature. If so, my joy will be misplaced, because it does not, after all, manifest one of my likes.

Moreover, not all emotional responses *directly* manifest a like or dislike, on this account. If I am dejected about the prospect of a hiking trip, this need not be because I dislike hiking as such. Rather, it may be that this particular trip threatens consequences (wet feet and wind chill) that I dislike. In this kind of case, then, I can explain why I am dejected about the trip: I am dejected because the trip is likely to involve wind chill and wet feet. In this kind of case, it is even easier to see that my emotional response might be misplaced. Perhaps the hike will be drier than I expect, or perhaps I am not as averse to soggy socks as I think. In either case, my response will fail to reflect the personal significance that the situation has for me.

I have argued, then, that the likes-based account does not present our emotional responses as concerned with trivialities, nor does it imply that they cannot be misplaced. Still, I have yet to explain why I prefer it to other possible accounts of personal significance. Indeed, it might be thought that this poses a particular problem for me. This is because, on the face of it, the teleosemantic theory points in just the opposite direction – away from a preference-based account and towards an interest-based account. In the next section, I shall explain why.

A Teleosemantic Argument for the Interest-Based Account?

Why might it be assumed that a teleosemanticist ought to endorse the interest-based account? To understand this, we need to recall the teleosemantic account presented earlier. On this account, the descriptive content of an emotional evaluation; depends on the answers to two questions:

- What conditions normally need to be in place if the emotional response is to perform its function effectively?
- What conditions is the evaluative system normally *able* to detect? In other words, what information is it normally sensitive to?

When we consider the second question, honours seem to be equal. The evaluative system may well have access to information about the subject's preferences. But, if so, it should have access to information about their interests too: for, as we saw earlier, people's preferences often *reflect* their interests. However, when we consider the first factor, the interest-based theory seems to do rather better. The reason has to do with a seemingly inconsequential point that I made in Chapter 3. I suggested there that the function of a biological organ or system is its *direct* contribution to other organs or systems in the body.

I have been assuming that our ancestors' capacity to experience personal emotions sometimes helped them to survive and produce healthy offspring. How, though, should we characterize this contribution? Should we say that it allowed our ancestors to cope with situations in which their preferences were at stake? Or should we refer, rather, to situations in which their interests were at stake? Perhaps we should say both these things. On the face of it, though, the most *direct* explanation is the one that refers to our ancestors' interests: for these were just the things they needed to thrive. If their preferences came into the story, this is only because their preferences sometimes *reflected* their interests; hence, by satisfying their preferences, they satisfied their interests too. But if this is right, the function of a sad or anxious response will relate to our interests, not our preferences. Hence, a teleosemanticist should conclude that the function of a sad or anxious evaluation₁ is to warn us that our interests are stake.

That, at least, is the argument. In the next section, I shall present two objections.

Unloved Interests and Idle Preferences

The first objection emerges when we consider what it means to say that a situation bears on someone's interests. Consider the case of a social recluse – call him Jay – who hates social contact of any kind. When his sister writes, proposing a visit, Jay sees no value in her coming, as he knows that he will not enjoy it. Still, it might be thought that it would be in his interests to see her: this is an opportunity for some much-needed social interaction. On closer examination, though, it is not clear that this is right. Certainly, there is a sense in which the visit offers Jay an opportunity for social interaction. Importantly, though, this is not an opportunity that he is able to exploit. Good social interaction is not a matter of going through the motions: it involves freely and willingly engaging in conversation, shared activities, and so on. Jay, though, is not in a position to freely engage in these things, and this is just because he takes no pleasure in doing them. As a result, he is not in a position to benefit from his sister's visit.

Similar points can be made about a wide range of cases. Reading *War and Peace*, for example, will not provide intellectual stimulation if you do not enjoy reading Russian novels; having some free time will not enhance your autonomy if there is nothing you want to do. What this suggests, then, is that we often cannot determine how a situation bears on someone's interests without taking their existing preferences into account. This is not because our interests themselves depend on our preferences; rather, it is because satisfying our interests often involves not only doing something, but doing it willingly or with pleasure.

If so, the argument I set out in the previous section is not quite right. In many cases, the *direct* contribution that our ancestors' emotional capacities made to their survival was not to help them to satisfy their interests full stop, but to help them to satisfy interests that they were already motivated to pursue, in ways in which they were already motivated to pursue them. This, by itself, does not show that the teleosemanticist should abandon the interest-based account. But it does imply that they should modify it: they should say, perhaps, that personal significance often depends not simply on the subject's interests, but on interests that they already value or care about. Modifying the account in this way, though, will bring it much closer to a preference-based account.

Nevertheless, even after this modification, the two accounts remain distinct. In particular, the interest-based theorist will continue to deny that *idle* preferences play any role in determining the personal significance of a situation: for idle preferences, by definition, are preferences for things that do not satisfy our interests. Moreover, it looks as if a teleosemanticist should side with the interest-based theorist on this. After all, how could our ancestors' emotional capacities have benefited them, biologically speaking, by helping them to satisfy merely idle preferences?

This point is not as decisive as it might appear. To see why, it helps to compare idle preferences with idle curiosity. Many people spend time investigating things that have no obvious practical use: they are curious about the workings of obsolete machinery or about the origins of the universe, without having any reason to think that this will help them to satisfy their interests. Nevertheless, it is highly plausible that this propensity has some biological utility. This is because, in a changing environment, information that is useless now might well come to be useful in the future, perhaps in some very unpredictable way.

Something similar may well be true of idle preferences too. Satisfying an idle preference has no biological utility now. Still, pursuing it might lead to the development of habits and skills that might well turn out be useful in the future. But if so, our ancestors could also have benefited from a propensity to get *emotional* about their idle preferences – to feel frustrated when some idle activity was interrupted or happy when they achieved some idle goal. If this is right, the teleosemanticist is not forced to deny that the personal significance of a situation might sometimes depend on an idle preference.

Where have we got to? I have argued that the teleosemanticist does have a strong reason to adopt at least a partly preference-based account. This is because, in many cases, how a situation impacts on the subject's interests will depend on their existing preferences. I have argued, too, that the teleosemantic theory is at least consistent with a purely preference-based theory. This is because it is possible that our ancestors benefited from a propensity to pursue idle preferences. Indeed, I am inclined to say something stronger than this: that this is a very plausible thing to think. If that is right, a teleosemanticist has some reason – albeit a speculative one – to lean towards a purely preference-based account.

Certainly, it does seem to be *intuitively* plausible to suppose that idle preferences have a bearing on the personal significance of the situation. Consider, for example, the case of

Kyra, who loves parachuting. Her love of parachuting, I shall suppose, is an idle preference: it does not help her to stay healthy, or contribute to her social life or provide intellectual stimulation. She simply enjoys the excitement of the jump. Recently, her doctor has told her that she must give up parachuting for the sake of her health. Kyra has accepted the advice, but is sad to give up an activity that she loves. Does Kyra's sorrow fit the situation? The most natural answer, it seems to me, is that it does. Even though her loss will not damage her interests, she is, nonetheless, being forced to give up something that she loves – something that is a source of great pleasure in her life. Intuitively, this is cause enough for her to feel sad. Certainly, it is hard to imagine that Kyra would be much comforted by the thought that her loss will not damage her interests.

As I mentioned at the start, it is not clear how much weight we should put on this kind of intuition. Arguably, though, this does provide some further support for a purely preference-based account.

Rival Preference-Based Accounts

The likes-based theorist faces a further objection. Even if there are reasons to suppose that personal significance depends on the subject's preferences, rather than their interests, this is not to say that it depends on their likes and dislikes. There are plenty of other ways in which it would be possible to develop a preference-based account.

One possible alternative has been developed by Helm (2001). Helm's account begins from a particular theory about the nature of evaluative rationality. According to Helm (2001: 60–98, 152–6), we are under a rational obligation to ensure that all our preferences – evaluative judgements, desires, emotional attitudes and likes – are mutually coherent, in the following sense: someone who judges something to be valuable without desiring it, or who desires something that they neither like nor value, is guilty of a kind of irrationality. On Helm's view, then, a fully rational person can be ascribed a single, overarching evaluative perspective, determined by all their preferences taken together: an emotional response will fit the situation only if it coheres with the subject's evaluative perspective overall (Helm, 2001: 125–60, 153). On Helm's account, then, the personal significance of a situation does not depend on a particular type of preference, but on preferences of every kind: likes, desires and values.[4]

I do not have space to do justice to Helm's broader account of evaluative rationality. What I want to focus on here is a particular implication of his account, namely the claim that personal significance depends, at least in part, on the subject's desires and values. We can envisage other preference-based accounts that imply similar claims: for example, it might be suggested that personal significance is wholly dependent on the subject's values.

How could we decide between these accounts? It is not clear that this issue can easily be settled by appealing to the teleosemantic theory. According to this theory, as we have seen, the descriptive content of an emotional evaluation$_i$ will depend on two things: the function of the emotional response that it is supposed to prompt; and the information that it normally carries. It is far from clear what we should say about the first consideration: certainly, a personal emotional response might function to help us to satisfy our likes; but there is no obvious reason to deny that its function might relate to other kinds of preference too.

At first glance, the second consideration is a much more promising avenue to explore. In particular, it might be thought, it might well provide a reason to deny that personal significance depends on the subject's values. For, as we saw in Chapter 5, emotional evaluations$_i$ seem to be independent of the subject's evaluative beliefs. This is, certainly, a relevant consideration; but it is not decisive. For even if emotional evaluations$_i$ do not *directly* depend on evaluative beliefs, it might be argued that they normally reflect them in some more roundabout way: perhaps the point of emotional education is to bring our emotional evaluations$_i$ into line with our values.

As far as the teleosemantic theory is concerned, then, which kind of preference-based theory to adopt remains an open question. Nevertheless, I would like to suggest that the likes-based account is at least more *plausible* than other kinds of preference-based account. To do this, I shall describe a case in which someone's likes are at odds with both their values and their desires. Suppose, then, that Leo is a television personality, a career he has pursued successfully for many years. Recently, he has become convinced that he should adopt a quieter, less demanding lifestyle. He no longer believes that excitement and worldly success are worth pursuing; rather, he values peace of mind. He now whole-heartedly wants to change his lifestyle. In fact, as his friends know, Leo loves his busy social life and the excitement of his job: if he gave it up, he would be wretched. Leo has just learned that a change in his circumstances makes it impossible for him to pursue his plan. He feels sad.

Does Leo's sorrow fit the situation? In this case, it seems to me, the answer is 'no'. The situation does not merit sorrow, but rather relief. This is because the success of his plan would have brought him nothing but misery. Of course, Leo himself has no reason to agree with this verdict. But this is only because he is mistaken about how his plan would impact upon his likes. It is easy, though, to imagine his friends telling him that his sorrow is misplaced; and that he should be feeling relieved at his lucky escape. Again, imagine that the situation changes, so that Leo is finally able to realize his plan, and is miserable as a result. In this situation, we might well imagine him recalling his sadness on this occasion, and realizing – ruefully – that it was misplaced.

If this is right, it tells in favour of the likes-based account. Someone who holds that the personal significance of the situation depends on Leo's desires or values should hold that his sorrow fits the situation, for the frustration of his plan deprives him of something that he values and wants. In contrast, the likes-based account implies that Leo's sorrow is misplaced: he has not lost anything that would bring him pleasure or joy.

On Helm's account, the issue is more complex. For Helm, the personal significance of the situation depends on Leo's evaluative perspective *overall*. One question, then, is whether Leo has a single evaluative perspective on the situation. According to Helm, this depends on how far his evaluative judgements about the situation are supported by his other preferences (Helm 2001: 150). Suppose, then, that Leo's preferences are sufficiently coherent to constitute a single evaluative perspective in favour of his plan: if so, Helm should suppose that his sorrow fits the situation. Alternatively, it may prove impossible to ascribe a single evaluative perspective to Leo. If so, Helm holds, it may simply be unclear what we should say (Helm 2001: 134–42). It seems to me, though, that the issue is not unclear: the fact that Leo has lost something that he wanted and valued does not seem to me to be *any* cause for sorrow, given that his desires and values reflect a mistaken assessment of his likes.

What if we tweak the example? We might imagine that Leo *realizes* that giving up his career will make him miserable, but that he wants to go ahead for the sake of some personal ideal. On this version of the story, it does seem more plausible that he has cause to feel sad about the frustration of his plan. But this need not be taken to imply that the personal significance of the situation depends directly on his desires or values. The explanation may be that Leo would take pleasure from satisfying his ideals: most people, after all, like to achieve things that they value. On this version of the story, then, even the likes-based theorist will think that Leo has *some* cause for sorrow. For the example to be helpful, we would need to suppose that Leo has only a cool, intellectual commitment to his ideal: this is, he thinks, something he ought to try to achieve, but it would give him no pleasure to do so. In this case, though, it seems rather less clear that he has cause to feel sad about the frustration of his plan. Certainly, I would not *expect* him to feel sad – a little frustrated perhaps, but also guiltily relieved.

Clearly, there is room for further discussion here. I am not claiming – far from it – to have settled the issue. I am suggesting only that consideration of this kind of case offers *some* reason to think that it is our likes, rather than our desires or values, that determine personal significance.

Summary

In the first part of this chapter, I offered a preliminary account of the intentional content of an emotional evaluation$_i$, drawing on a teleosemantic theory of content. In doing this, I explored some ways in which its content might be thought to reflect the structure and function of the emotional response that it functions to prompt. This account, though, omitted something important: it failed to address the problem of emotional significance. In the second part of this chapter, I tried to make good this omission – at least for personal emotional responses. For these cases, I suggested, albeit tentatively, that the personal significance of a situation depends on the subject's likes and dislikes. I argued that this view is at least consistent with a teleosemantic theory, and that it has some intuitive plausibility. In what follows, I shall explore some further implications of this account.

Further Reading

If you are interested in exploring teleosemantic theories, you might start with Karen Neander's (2012) entry on 'Teleological theories of mental content' in the *Stanford Encyclopedia of Philosophy*. For some attempts to apply this kind of theory to emotional evaluations, see Prinz (2004: Chap. 3); Price (2006a). Accounts of emotional significance are offered by Ben Ze'ev (2000: 18–21); Helm (2001: esp. Chap. 5); Nussbaum (2001: Chap. 1); Baier (2004); Price (2013). For the role of pleasure and pain in grounding our preferences, see Millgram (1993).

6
The Rationality of Emotion

Introduction

'My heart says one thing; my head another.' The idea that 'head' – representing reason – and 'heart' – representing emotion – stand in opposition is familiar enough. Indeed, in earlier chapters, I have said some things that might seem to favour this picture: in Chapter 5, for example, I argued that emotional evaluations₁ are not judgements or beliefs; and in Chapter 6, I presented a picture of personal evaluations₁ as answering to our likes and dislikes, rather than our considered values. All this might be taken to support a view of emotion as distinct from – and sometimes at odds with – our reason.

On the other hand, ordinary ways of talking about emotion do not always assume a rigid divide between emotion and reason. As we saw in Chapter 5, people often talk as if they have reasons for their emotional responses. Moreover, emotional responses are sometimes said to be irrational, implying that they can be judged by rational standards. In this chapter, I shall examine these claims. In doing this, I shall revisit the questions that I raised in Chapter 5. In what ways are emotional evaluations₁ similar to perceptions? How far can we take this comparison? I shall end by considering cases in which someone's emotional responses conflict not with their judgements, but with each other. What does this phenomenon tell us about the 'logic' of emotion?

Emotional Recalcitrance

Recalcitrance and Irrationality

As we saw in Chapter 5, emotional evaluations; sometimes clash with our considered judgements. Many people feel disgusted at the thought of drinking apple juice that has been touched by a (sterilized) cockroach, even though they do not believe that it is contaminated; someone might be afraid of flying, but travel by plane anyway, because they do not believe that flying is particularly dangerous. These are cases of recalcitrant emotion.

As we saw in Chapter 5, the phenomenon of recalcitrant emotion poses a problem for theorists who hold that emotional evaluations; are evaluative judgements. This is because emotional recalcitrance is not plausibly viewed as a clash of judgements. In contrast, perception theorists offer another, apparently more plausible, comparison: cases of emotional recalcitrance, they suggest, can be compared to cases of conflict between judgement and perception. Perception theorists often compare cases of emotional recalcitrance to cases involving optical illusion, such as the Müller–Lyer illusion. In these cases, the subject's perception persists in the face of their judgement, just as the emotional evaluation; persists in a case of emotional recalcitrance (Prinz, 2008: 157–8; Döring, 2009; Tappolet, 2012). In Chapter 5, I gave the example of seeing a toy spade half-submerged in a paddling pool: I see the spade's handle as crooked, but I do not believe that it is.

As I mentioned in Chapter 5, however, it is also possible to find an apparent contrast between recalcitrant emotional responses and these perceptual cases. Recalcitrant emotions are often described as irrational. Yet, perceptual experiences that conflict with the subject's beliefs are not described in this way: it is not irrational to see a spade handle as crooked even when you know that it is straight (Helm, 2001: 42). As I explained in Chapter 5, this does not constitute an objection to the weak perception view: weak perception theorists hold that emotional evaluations; are like perceptions in important ways; but they need not suppose that they are like them in every way. On the face of it, though, this does constitute an objection to the strong perception view: strong perception theorists hold that emotional evaluations are *literally* perceptions of some kind. We might wonder, then, how a strong perception theorist might respond to this objection. More generally, this phenomenon seems to be in need of explanation: given that cases of emotional recalcitrance do seem to be similar to cases of perceptual illusion, it is rather puzzling that we seem to judge them by different standards.

This issue has received plenty of attention in recent years. I shall start by considering two responses, one suggested by Michael Brady (2007, 2009) and the other by Christine Tappolet (2012). Both these solutions might be viewed as attempts to explain this difference in a way that is compatible with the strong perception view. Indeed, Tappolet explicitly endorses the suggestion that emotional evaluations are perceptions (see also D'Arms and Jacobson, 2003; Roberts, 2003: 91–3; Döring, 2007, 2009). In contrast, Brady himself does not endorse this view (Brady, 2013): he is considering only how a strong perception theorist *might* respond to the problem.[1]

To understand Brady's solution, it helps to begin with a particular example. Consider the case of Meg, who suffers from a recalcitrant fear of flying. As she sits on a plane, waiting for take-off, she has to steel herself to remain in her seat. The changes that are happening in her body are priming her to take action (to flee, say); meanwhile, her attention is focused on the (apparent) dangers of the situation – for example, her helplessness should anything go wrong. Brady makes two points about this. First, these changes constitute a *waste* of Meg's bodily and cognitive resources. Recalcitrant emotion, Brady suggests, is 'the equivalent of preparing for an interview that one has already had, or of training for a race that one has already run' (Brady, 2007: 281). Secondly, and more importantly, Meg's emotional response is *epistemically* risky: in her fear, Meg's attention is focused on the apparent dangers of the situation, and away from the statistical evidence (say) that supports her evaluative belief. As a result, she may well be strongly tempted to judge that she *is*, in fact, in some danger (Brady, 2009: 424–5). Both these considerations, Brady thinks, constitute reasons for Meg to try to overcome her fear. In contrast, when I see the spade handle as crooked, my visual experience does not dominate my attention or prime me to act; nor does it tempt me to believe that the handle is crooked. I simply note the anomaly and move on.

Brady is surely right to point out that we often have good reasons to try to overcome a recalcitrant emotion (see also Price, 2010: 28; Döring, 2010: 298). However, I am not convinced that he has succeeded in explaining why cases of recalcitrant emotion differ from cases involving perception. The difficulty emerges when we think not about visual or auditory experiences, but about bodily feelings, such as pain and hunger. Pain and hunger capture our attention and prime us to act in much the way that emotional responses do. Arguably, they have epistemic significance too: certainly, when I am hungry, I am strongly tempted to believe that I need food; when I am in pain, I am strongly tempted to believe that I have been hurt. Moreover, bodily feelings sometimes conflict with the subject's beliefs. People who lose an arm, for example, sometimes feel as if their arm is hurting, even though they know that it is no longer there. Similarly, someone with an appetite disorder might experience hunger pangs, despite knowing that they do not need to eat. Hence on Brady's account, we should expect to find that these feelings, too, strike us as irrational. But this seems wrong: phantom pain is illusory and damaging, but it is not irrational. This looks like a problem for this account.

While Brady's solution focuses on the effects produced by emotional evaluations, Tappolet focuses on their causes. According to Tappolet, the difference between Meg's case and the spade case is that Meg has the capacity to *change* her emotional response. Even if Meg cannot do very much about her fearful reaction now, in the longer term, she may be able to eradicate her fear – perhaps by engaging in some kind of behavioural or cognitive therapy. This, Tappolet thinks, is an important difference between emotion and sense perception, such as sight or hearing. We cannot usually get rid of our susceptibility to optical or auditory illusions: people cannot learn, for example, to compensate for the effects of refraction, or to see through the Müller–Lyer illusion. Moreover, Tappolet suggests, this explains why it makes sense to describe recalcitrant emotional responses as irrational: they are irrational because they are the product of an emotional susceptibility that the subject should, and could, eliminate (Tappolet, 2012: 220–1).

As I shall explain later, I agree that the educability of emotion plays an important role in explaining why recalcitrant emotional evaluations are often taken to be irrational (see also Price, 2012a: 227). Nevertheless, I am not convinced that educability alone is the solution. For while Tappolet is right to point out that certain basic features of our perceptual mechanisms cannot be changed, this does not seem to be true of more complex recognitional capacities. These might include, for example, the ability to hear a sequence of sounds as the word 'bubble', to recognize a friend's face or to recognize the smell of coffee. These recognitional capacities are learned; and, in some cases, they can be unlearned too.

As an example, consider a case of misheard song lyrics. For many years I was puzzled by a line in Bob Dylan's song 'It's All Over Now, Baby Blue'. Each time I listened to the song, I heard Dylan sing, 'Take what you have gathered from going so dense.' I did not *believe* that was what he was singing: Dylan's lyrics are not usually that peculiar. Still, I could not help hearing the line that way, presumably because my auditory mechanisms had no better hypothesis to offer. Eventually, a friend explained that what sounded like 'going so dense' was, in fact, 'coincidence'. I set out to retrain myself to hear the line correctly; it took several attempts, but eventually I began to hear the line differently.

On the face of it, this is a case of conflict between perception and belief: my perception clashed, first, with my belief that Dylan could not have been singing 'going so dense'; and, for a short period later on, with my belief that he was in fact singing 'coincidence'. In this case, though, I was able to resolve the conflict by re-educating my perceptual habits. On Tappolet's account, then, we should feel inclined to describe my recalcitrant auditory experience as irrational. This, though, does not seem right: on the face of it, my auditory experience was not irrational, just mistaken.

The worry raised by this case, then, is that educability is not sufficient to explain why cases of recalcitrant emotion are sometimes described as irrational: something else is needed. Before I can make my own suggestion, however, I first need to consider another issue that I raised in Chapter 5: the idea that we can have *reasons* or *grounds* for our emotional responses. I am going to argue that we can make sense of this idea. I want to suggest, too, that this can help us to understand why we are often inclined to describe recalcitrant emotional responses as irrational. I shall begin by recalling one of the contrasts between judgements and perceptions that I drew in Chapter 5 – responsiveness to reasoning.

Grounds for Emotion

Reasons and Grounds

Suppose that I am listening to a busker playing a violin: I quickly form the judgement that her violin is out of tune. If challenged, I will almost certainly be able to say why I have this belief: some of the notes sound flat. Once I have identified my evidence for forming this judgement, I can ask whether it is *good* evidence; I can weigh it up in the light of other things that I believe. Perhaps I remember that violins always sound out of tune to me, even when they are not. If so, I may realize that my judgement is not well grounded, and so might not be true. If I realize this, rationality requires that I should reconsider.

Now suppose that someone asks me why I hear a particular note as flat. In this case, the situation is very different. As we saw in Chapter 5, my auditory experience is produced by psychological systems that operate outside conscious awareness. As a result, I am unlikely to be in a position to identify the cues that these mechanisms are exploiting, or to evaluate whether my auditory experience properly reflects the information reaching my ears. The cues to which I am responding are not considerations that I can weigh up and evaluate: they do not constitute *reasons* to experience the music in that way.

Where do emotional evaluations_i fit into this picture? Consider Bill's fearful evaluation_i of Monty. In order to produce that evaluation_i, Bill must first have seen Monty; he must have recognized him *as* Monty, or at least as a snake – a creature he takes to be dangerous; he must have assessed Monty's distance and speed. He may also be drawing on information about other features of the situation: perhaps he remembers that he heard Yolanda's car leaving a few minutes ago, leaving him alone with Monty; perhaps a heavy cold is making him feel particularly vulnerable. This evaluative process does not itself involve conscious deliberation or inference; nevertheless, it seems to draw on information of which Bill is himself aware – things that he perceives, remembers or believes. As a result, Bill may well be able to identify – though perhaps only after some reflection – the cues that prompted his evaluation$_i$.

I do not want to insist that this is true in every case. It might turn out that some emotional evaluations$_i$ are produced at such an early stage of processing that it is impossible for the subject to identify the cues involved. A sudden movement, say, might strike you as frightening in the very moment you become aware of it. I am claiming only that we are often able to identify some of the considerations that support our emotional evaluations$_i$.

If so, this has an important consequence: it means that we are often in a position to consider whether the features that have prompted an evaluation$_i$ constitute a *good* basis for our emotional reaction. Moreover, there is some point in asking this question. This is because the answer may be able to influence our emotional responses. In some cases – cases in which someone notices that they have made some simple factual error – their emotional response might dissipate at once. In many cases, though, it is the subject's emotional susceptibilities that are at fault. As we have seen, people's emotional susceptibilities can be educated: Bill, for example, might try to reduce his fear of Monty by becoming accustomed to seeing and handling him. In this way, he can ensure that his fearful responses are sensitive to the right cues. He can ensure, in other words, that his fearful responses are well grounded, just as he might ensure that he has good reasons for a judgement (cf. Brady, 2007: 275–6; 2013: 112–13).

I do not want to press this analogy too far. Our judgements are directly and immediately responsive to our reasons: if I recognize that I do not have good evidence that the busker's violin is out of tune, this should prompt me to revise my belief straightaway. In contrast, as I emphasized in Chapter 5, retraining our emotional susceptibilities can be a slow and indirect process. The two cases, then, are not exactly analogous. Rather, emotion could be seen as occupying a position midway between perception and judgement. In what follows, I will mark this point by making a terminological distinction: beliefs and judgements, I shall say, are responsive to reasons; emotional evaluations₁ characteristically rest on *grounds*.

perception ⌐emotion⌐ judg.

Three Objections

In this section, I shall consider, and try to fend off, three objections that might be raised to the view that I have just presented. I shall begin with the simplest and easiest to answer.

The first objection is that there is an inconsistency between the picture I presented in the previous section and the claim – which I endorsed in Chapter 5 – that emotional evaluations₁ are independent of our judgements and beliefs. In the previous section, I allowed that Bill's grounds for fearing Monty might include things that he believes. Does this not imply, then, that his fearful response depends (at least in part) on a belief? This worry is relatively easy to answer, once we remember the distinction between evaluative beliefs and non-evaluative beliefs, which I drew in Chapter 5. In Chapter 5, I drew a distinction between Bill's evaluative judgement that Monty is dangerous and his fearful evaluation₁. I suggested that these are different kinds of intentional states, which are produced by independent processes of evaluation. But this is perfectly consistent with the claim that Bill's fearful evaluation₁ may well be grounded, in part, on his *non-evaluative* beliefs – for example, the belief that pythons are capable of killing people (cf. Brady, 2013: 113).

Secondly, it might be objected that I have misunderstood what we ordinarily mean when we talk about reasons for emotion. Suppose that Bill is discussing his fearful response to Monty with a rather unsympathetic friend. Defending his reaction, Bill insists that, given Monty's size and strength, he had good grounds for fear. It is not obvious that Bill is referring to considerations that *ground* his fearful evaluation₁. He might mean, rather, that these are features *in virtue of which* Monty is dangerous. If so, Monty's size and strength help to justify Bill's fear, not because they constitute grounds for fear, but because they imply that his fearful evaluation; fits the situation (cf. Tappolet, 2012: 215–16).

This, though, does not seem right, for a number of reasons. Monty may have other dangerous traits – speed, for example – which also help to explain why Bill's fearful response fits the situation. This is not to say, however, that Monty's speed constitutes grounds for Bill's fearful evaluation;. To describe it in this way implies that Bill is actually *aware* that Monty can move very quickly, and that this, in turn, helps to explain why he is afraid. Conversely, to describe Bill's fear as well grounded does not by itself imply that it fits the situation. Monty's size and strength might still constitute good *grounds* for Bill to fear him, even if, unknown to Bill, Monty is not in a mood to attack. Finally, Bill's grounds need not be limited to Monty's dangerous features. They might include the fact that Monty is staring at him and flickering his tongue – behaviours that Bill takes to be a sign of aggression. These are not features in virtue of which Monty is dangerous, but rather evidence that he is. There is no reason to think, then, that the claim that Bill's fearful evaluation; is well grounded is equivalent to the claim that it fits the situation.

Thirdly, it might be objected that I have overestimated the dissimilarity between emotion and perception. It is true, the objector might concede, that in many cases of perception, I am not aware of the cues that my perceptual systems are exploiting: I may not be able to say why I hear a particular note as flat or why I see a line as straight. But this is not true in every case. Consider, for example, what happens when I see something as an elephant: in this case, I can easily identify many of the features – shape, size, colour, gait – that explain why the creature looks like an elephant. Moreover, this kind of recognitional capacity is educable: I may well be able to improve my elephant-spotting skills. On the face of it, then, this looks very similar to a case of emotion, as I have described it. It might seem, then, that, on my account, we ought to say that the object's size, colour, and so on, constitute my grounds for seeing it as an elephant.

I want to suggest, though, that there is a difference between the two cases. When I see something as an elephant, this does not involve two separate visual experiences, one of which provides grounds for the other: I do not see it as large, grey, and so on, and also, separately, see it as an elephant. Rather, my seeing the object as an elephant is *constituted* by my seeing it as having elephant-like features, organized in a particular way. It is a matter of recognizing a familiar – if perhaps rather abstract – visual *pattern*.

Producing an emotional evaluation might also be thought to involve identifying a pattern: I need to recognize the situation as embodying a certain kind of *scenario* – for example, one in which I am at risk of significant injury, or one in which I have just suffered a significant loss. To do this, I may need to combine many different pieces of information – information about the situation, about my own condition, about my likes and dislikes. More importantly, I may need to draw on several different *sources* of information: bodily feelings, external sense perceptions, memories and background beliefs might all come into play. In this case, however, the evaluation that results is not *identical* to any of these states: for, as I argued in Chapter 5, an emotional evaluation is not itself a sense perception, or a bodily feeling or a belief. It is a further representation, distinct from the perceptions, memories and (non-evaluative) beliefs that prompt it. There are, then, two (sets of) representations here, one of which provides grounds for the other.

Good Grounds

I have suggested that emotional evaluations are sometimes supported by grounds. What, though, constitutes *good* grounds for an emotional response? Patricia Greenspan has argued that emotional evaluations and judgements are governed by different standards of evidence: while our judgements should be sensitive to all the evidence we have, emotional evaluations are responses to just a *part* of the available evidence. For an emotional response to be well grounded, in her view, it is enough that it is supported by just *some* significant facts (Greenspan, 1980: 237; 1988: 87–8).

How might we assess this suggestion? Throughout this book, I have appealed to functional considerations to settle important questions about emotion. I shall adopt the same approach here: what constitutes good grounds for an emotional evaluation$_i$, I shall assume, depends on its function and on how it is normally produced. Greenspan adopts a similar approach: in arguing for her conclusion, she appeals to the idea that our emotional capacities are *adaptive*, in the sense that they help us to secure our interests (Greenspan, 1988: 7–14, 83–107). Claims about adaptiveness are not exactly equivalent to claims about function: in particular, adaptiveness is not a historical notion. Nevertheless, Greenspan and I agree that the standards by which we judge emotional evaluations$_i$ should take account of the role that emotion plays (or, on my view, that it is *supposed* to play) in our psychology. Moreover, I agree that, if we take this line, we can indeed find reasons to think that emotional evaluations$_i$ and judgements answer to different standards of evidence. I shall suggest three ways in which this might come about.

First, it is sometimes suggested that the mechanisms that produce emotional evaluations$_i$ often operate on a hair trigger (Griffiths, 1997: 95). Given the function of an emotional evaluation$_i$, this makes sense. Its job is to ensure that the subject responds effectively to some significant challenge or opportunity; overlooking such a situation might well have damaging consequences – more damaging, often, than the consequences of being over-sensitive. Moreover, in some cases, the subject needs to respond to the situation very quickly: this is true in the case of fear and disgust, for example. This suggests that an emotional evaluation$_i$ is not supposed to embody the subject's considered assessment of the situation; it is a rough-and-ready, 'first blush' appraisal – an alarm bell, which goes off at the first signs of trouble (cf. Greenspan, 1988: 93–4; Baier, 2004: 200). If so, it seems reasonable to conclude that what constitutes adequate evidence for an emotional evaluation$_i$ may be less than is required for an evaluative judgement.

There is, though, an important proviso. The point is most convincing if we are thinking of someone's *initial* emotional reaction. The longer the subject's emotional response continues, the more opportunity they will have to evaluate$_i$ the situation more carefully. On the other hand, in these cases, there is time for a second factor to come into play: the propensity of an emotional response to focus the subject's attention on particular aspects of the situation and to direct it away from others. This narrowing of attention is not just an unfortunate side-effect of an emotional response, but is integral to its function. Hence, even in the longer term, an emotional evaluation; will not normally draw on the same breadth of evidence as an evaluative judgement.

Thirdly, we might consider the *sources* of information on which emotional evaluations; are based (Price, 2012a: 226). In many cases, emotional evaluations; seem to be particularly sensitive to perception, memory and imagination. For example, suppose that you know that, in a short while, you will have to cross an old rope bridge, slung across a deep gorge. You have been told about the bridge, and you know that the crossing will be a dangerous one. But it is only when you *see* the bridge, swaying precariously over the dizzying drop, that you feel fear. It is not that you have learned something new: the bridge is no narrower, no feebler than you believed. But it is only when you *see* the bridge that the danger really strikes you. This, I would suggest, is a familiar feature of emotional responses. One can firmly believe that the accident at the roundabout was horrific; or that one's missing relative has been found safe and well; or that one has made a fool of oneself. But it is not until one *sees* the wreckage, or *hears* the voice on the telephone, *remembers* or *imagines* the mocking laughter, that emotion takes hold.

I have suggested, then, three reasons for thinking that emotional evaluations; may answer to lower standards of evidence than judgements and beliefs. It is worth bearing in mind, though, that these considerations may not apply equally to all types of emotion. Not all emotions are 'emergency' emotions like fear or disgust; conceivably, not all types of emotion are equally sensitive to perceptual information. Hence, it might turn out that what constitutes a well-grounded emotional response depends on which type of emotion we have in mind.

Recalcitrance and Grounds

In this section, I have been discussing one significant respect in which emotional evaluations; might be thought to *contrast* with perceptions: we characteristically have grounds for our emotional evaluations$_i$. Earlier, I considered another apparent contrast between emotion and perception: recalcitrant emotional responses are often described as irrational. I want to suggest that these two features of emotion are connected.

Suppose that I believe that you have stolen my favourite teaspoon: I have no good evidence for this; moreover, it should be obvious to me that my belief is unjustified. But I cling to it, nonetheless. This looks like a clear case of irrationality. My belief is irrational because it is obviously unjustified. Cases of recalcitrant emotion, I want to suggest, often have a similar structure: they are cases in which the subject is in a position to recognize that their emotional evaluation$_i$ is not only misplaced, but also poorly grounded. Consider, for example, the case of Rozin's subjects. They were well aware that they did not have good grounds for disgust: contact with a sterilized cockroach is not evidence of contamination. There is an analogy, then, between this case and the case of irrational belief described above. It is this analogy, I want to suggest, that we are invoking when we describe cases of recalcitrant emotion as irrational (cf. Brady, 2013: 112).

The educability of emotions plays an important role in this explanation. For, as we have seen, the claim that our emotional evaluations$_i$ can be well or poorly grounded presupposes that our emotional susceptibilities can be educated. To this extent, then, I agree with Tappolet. On my account, though, educability is only half the story. It matters, too, that the subject's emotional evaluation$_i$ is grounded on their existing perceptions, memories and beliefs. This is why cases of recalcitrant emotion differ from the spade handle case.

It might be thought, though, that there is something odd about my explanation: after all, the conflict involved in these cases arises because the subject has reason to believe that their emotional evaluation$_i$ is *misplaced*, not just poorly grounded. It seems natural to assume, then, that it is this that we have in mind when we describe the subject's emotional response as irrational. However, although the first claim is surely right, I am not convinced that the conclusion follows.

Moreover, there may be a way to put this to the test. Earlier, I suggested that emotional evaluations$_i$ and evaluative beliefs may well answer to different standards of evidence.

This raises an interesting possibility: there might be some cases of recalcitrant emotion in which the subject has adequate grounds *both* for their evaluative belief *and* for their emotional evaluation$_i$. In this case, on my account, the subject's emotional response will be recalcitrant, but it will not be irrational. This is because the conflict between the subject's belief and their emotional response does not imply that the emotional response is poorly grounded. Arguably, it is possible to find examples of this phenomenon. Consider, for example, the following case. Suppose that Nadim is standing at the doorway of an aeroplane, about to take his first parachute jump. He confidently believes that the jump will be safe – otherwise, he would not be willing to go through with it. Suppose, too, that he has good evidence for this belief: the instructors are highly experienced and well trained, and nobody has ever been seriously injured at this school. Nevertheless, as he contemplates the stupendous drop below and feels the wind violently tugging at his clothes, he feels afraid.

Nadim has good reasons to believe that his fear is misplaced. Hence, he would do well to try to *overcome* his fear, for all the reasons that Brady (2007, 2009) identifies. Given the circumstances, though, his fear does not strike me as *irrational*, exactly. After all, the situation looks and feels extremely dangerous. Moreover, if the account I have offered here is correct, it is easy to see why this might not strike us as a case of irrational fear. Nadim's feelings are not a product of faulty susceptibilities: the look and feel of the situation provide more than adequate grounds for fear, even if, in this case, appearances happen to be misleading. If this is right, it lends some support to the claim that our readiness to describe recalcitrant emotional responses as irrational depends, not on the assumption that the subject's response is misplaced, but rather on the assumption that it is poorly grounded.

Assessing the Strong Perception View

I have been considering some ways in which emotional evaluations$_i$ might be thought to contrast with perceptions, and I have suggested that these contrasts can, in fact, be drawn. We can make sense of the idea that people have grounds for their emotional evaluations$_i$, and having done this, we can explain what people are getting at when they describe cases of recalcitrant emotion as irrational. Where does this leave the strong perception view?

There does, I think, remain some room for debate about this. It might still be suggested that the similarities between emotion and perception outweigh the contrasts; and that they do so to such an extent that we are justified in treating emotional evaluations$_i$ as a class of perceptions, albeit one with some unusual features. My own view is that the contrasts are significant enough to warrant retreating to the weak perception view. Emotional evaluations$_i$ are like perceptions in important ways: most importantly, they are not directly responsive to reasoning, in the way that judgements are. But, while it seems natural to think of perception as our first contact with the world, our emotional evaluations$_i$ often depend on what we already perceive, remember or believe. This seems to me to be reason enough to place them in a class of their own.

The Authority of Emotion

Earlier, I suggested that we characteristically have grounds for our emotional evaluations$_i$. Often, then, we are in a position to justify our feelings, and where we cannot do so, we may be in a position to take steps – albeit slow and indirect – to set things right. This raises a further question about the relative authority of emotion and belief. When belief and emotion conflict, we tend to assume that it is the emotional response, not the belief, which requires adjustment (Helm, 2001; 146–7; Döring, 2009: 246). Why, though, should this be? And does it imply that we have nothing to learn from our emotional evaluations$_i$?

I raised this question, albeit briefly, in Chapter 6. As I mentioned, the issue depends, in part, on what our emotional evaluations$_i$ are about. Are they concerned with things that we care about, or have reason to care about? This depends, in turn, on what we take emotional significance to be. In Chapter 6, I suggested that, for many of our personal emotional responses, emotional significance seems to depend on the subject's likes and dislikes. With this view comes a certain picture of the role that these responses play in our personal lives: they should be viewed as advocates for a particular *subset* of our concerns. As I emphasized in Chapter 6, our likes and dislikes are not mere passing fancies: they are fundamental concerns of ours, rooted both in our needs as biological and social beings and in our experiences of the world. But they are not *all* that matters to us. In particular, they can clash with our considered values and ideals; they can clash with our interests too. We might think of our emotional evaluations$_i$ as representing a particular perspective on the situation. It is a perspective that we would do well to take seriously; sometimes, though – when important values or interests are stake – we may have good reason to disregard it.

The issue, however, does not depend only on this. It also depends on the relative reliability of emotion and belief. I have argued that our evaluative judgements and our emotional evaluations$_i$ are produced by different evaluative processes. Moreover, I have suggested that the processes that produce emotional evaluations$_i$ may well work to a lower standard of evidence than the processes that produce our beliefs. If this is right, our emotional evaluations$_i$ will tend to be less reliable than our evaluative beliefs, even when it comes to indicating the personal significance of the situation.[2]

It is important not to overstate this point. After all, things do not always go as they normally should: our evaluative judgements can be hasty, biased, self-interested or confused. In particular cases, it may well be our emotional response, not our reasoned judgement, that gets things right. Moreover, if the account that I have given is correct, our evaluative beliefs and our emotional evaluations$_i$ may sometimes reflect rather different bodies of evidence. Our emotional evaluations$_i$ embody lessons from our past, from our evolutionary history and from our personal experiences – including, perhaps, childhood experiences that we have now forgotten; and they are particularly strongly influenced by perception, memory and imagination. It is possible, then, that they sometimes reflect important features of the situation that we might otherwise overlook.

I have suggested, then, that our personal emotional responses reflect a particular set of concerns and a particular body of information. As a result, the verdicts implied by our evaluative beliefs will tend to be more balanced and better supported. The moral to draw, though, is not that our emotional evaluations$_i$ never have the power to challenge our beliefs: conflict between emotion and judgement may yet be a sign that something important has been missed. The wise course is neither to dismiss our emotional response nor to follow our hearts, but to stop and think again (cf. Helm, 2001: 147).

Emotional Ambivalence

Introducing Ambivalence

For much of this chapter, we have been considering cases in which emotion conflicts with belief. There is, though, another form of emotional conflict that we might consider: cases in which our emotional responses conflict with each other. This phenomenon is sometimes labelled 'emotional ambivalence'. As the term is used in the philosophical literature, emotional ambivalence occurs when both the following conditions are met.

- A person's emotional response to a particular aspect of the situation involves two or more distinct types of emotional evaluation$_i$.
- At least one of these evaluations$_i$ implies that this aspect of the situation has *positive* emotional significance for the subject; at least one implies that it has *negative* emotional significance.

Suppose, for example, that Orson (a young man just starting out in life) has run up a large debt. Penny (Orson's well-meaning but overbearing mother) has repaid the debt herself, without consulting him. When Orson finds out, he feels grateful to her for stepping in, but also resentful about her intervention. This may well be a case of emotional ambivalence.

To be sure that it is, we need to describe the case quite carefully. First, it must be the case that Orson feels grateful and resentful *at the same time*: otherwise, we should say that Orson's emotions are fluctuating, rather than ambivalent. Secondly, it is important that Orson's gratitude and his resentment are *about the same aspect of the situation*. Suppose, for example, that Orson is grateful that Penny helped him, but resentful that she did not consult him first: in this case, Orson's emotions concern different aspects of the situation, and so are not ambivalent. To describe his response as ambivalent implies that he is both grateful for and resentful *about the same thing* – for example, the fact that Penny stepped in to help (Greenspan, 1980). To characterize Orson's response as ambivalent, then, is to imply that he has made two opposing evaluations$_i$ of the situation: his gratitude implies that his mother's intervention has *benefited* him; while his resentment implies that it has *harmed* him. It might be argued, then, that he ought to choose between these evaluations$_i$: harbouring both is inconsistent and therefore irrational.

My own view, in contrast, is that Orson's ambivalence is *not* irrational (though, as I shall explain later on, there are cases in which I take a different view). Someone who takes this line, however, needs to explain how this can be the right thing to say. After all, if Orson knowingly harboured inconsistent *beliefs* about Penny's behaviour, this would be irrational. Why is emotional ambivalence any different?

I shall approach this question by considering Patricia Greenspan's account of ambivalence. Greenspan (1980, 1988) also denies that emotional ambivalence always involves some kind of irrationality, and she sets out to explain why. I want to suggest that her account is not quite right. Seeing why, though, will help us to reach a better understanding of how ambivalence arises, and why it is not always irrational. To understand Greenspan's account, it will help to start by recalling the account of personal significance that I presented in Chapter 6.

Greenspan: Ambivalence and Evidence

What makes a loss a *sad* loss? What makes a success a *joyous* success? In Chapter 6, I suggested that, in the case of personal emotional responses, we should accept the following claim:

P   Emotionally significant situations are ones that bear on the subject's personal concerns.

I suggested, too, that there is some reason to think that, in this context, the concerns that matter are the subject's likes and dislikes. Here, though, the issue does not rest on what *kinds* of concern determine emotional significance, but on another potential point of controversy. For, as I mentioned briefly in Chapter 6, P contains a further ambiguity. It might mean either of the following things:

P1   Emotionally significant situations are ones that bear on the subject's personal concerns *overall*.

P2   Emotionally significant situations are ones that bear on *one or more* of the subject's personal concerns.

Greenspan adopts something like P1. She holds that emotional evaluations$_i$ are unqualified 'all-out' assessments of the situation. On her view, Orson's gratitude implies that Penny has benefited him *full stop*; his resentment implies that she has harmed him *full stop*. Hence these two evaluations$_i$ contradict each other.

   Why, then, does Greenspan think that Orson can rationally harbour both? Her answer relies on a claim that we met earlier: the claim that emotional evaluations$_i$ answer to a lower standard of evidence than evaluative judgements. Emotional evaluations$_i$, she thinks, are not carefully considered, nuanced assessments of the situation. Rather, they are rough-and-ready, 'first blush' appraisals, which are justified so long as there is *some* evidence in their favour. As she puts it, they are 'typically "all-out" reactions to *portions* of the evidence' (Greenspan, 1988: 87–8, italics in the original). Consider, for example, Orson's grateful evaluation$_i$ of Penny's behaviour. For this to be well grounded, according to Greenspan, Orson need not have decisive evidence that Penny's action benefited him, but only some evidence to that effect. Similarly, his resentful evaluation$_i$ will be adequately grounded provided that he has some evidence that Penny's action has harmed him. It is perfectly possible, then, that Orson has adequate grounds for both evaluations$_i$.

As my earlier discussion made clear, I am sympathetic to the view that emotional evaluations$_i$ answer to lower standards of evidence than judgements. However, I am not sure that this is the right way to explain emotional ambivalence. Certainly, Greenspan's explanation comes at a cost. For while she can allow that Orson's gratitude and resentment are both adequately supported by the evidence, her account appears to imply that at least one must be misplaced. For it cannot be the case that the effect of Penny's action is both negative and positive full stop. Hence, although Greenspan can allow that Orson's ambivalent response is not irrational, it does imply that he ought to be suspicious of it: he should know, when he reflects on it, that it is at least partly misplaced.

Emotional Ambivalence: An Alternative View

There is another way in which we might accommodate the view that emotional ambivalence is not always irrational: we can adopt P2. On this view, Orson's gratitude implies that Penny's intervention has benefited him *in some respect*; his resentment implies that it has harmed him *in some respect*. On this reading, it is possible that both evaluations$_i$ fit the situation: Penny's action may well bear positively on one of Orson's likes but negatively on another (cf. Tappolet, 2005).

Why does Greenspan reject this suggestion? This is because she takes it to imply that emotional responses depend on complex, nuanced appraisals of the situation (Greenspan, 1980: 233). However, I do not think that this follows from P2. Consider, for example, Orson's grateful evaluation$_i$: we do not need to suppose that this involves an assessment of *how* exactly Penny's action has benefited him. It implies only that Penny's action has benefited him in some respect or other. This does not look like a particularly sophisticated assessment.

There is a second reason someone might have to favour P1 over P.2. It might be suggested that a rational person should ensure that their preferences are *coherent*, in the sense that it is possible to realize them all together. Suppose, for example, that I like being rich and that I also like being honest: the world being as it is and my talents being as they are, I cannot have both these things. It might be suggested, then, that it is irrational for me to continue liking both: I should cultivate different tastes. But if my likes are coherent in this sense, something that promotes one of my likes will promote my likes overall. So long as we are rational, then, P2 will *imply* P1.

It is far from clear, though, why we should think that rational people should ensure that their preferences are coherent in this sense. The idea might be that this kind of coherence is required for effective agency: having incoherent preferences makes it impossible to decide what to do. But this seems false. Characteristically, our practical decisions are shaped by a host of considerations: conflict between two of them is unlikely to lead to paralysis. Moreover, it is quite possible that I will never need to choose between my conflicting likes: perhaps I will never have the opportunity to pursue great wealth, honestly or not. Moreover, since I cannot predict what opportunities will come my way, it makes sense to leave my options open (Rorty, 2010). Hence, we need not think that our preferences ought to be coherent in this strong sense.[3]

I have suggested, then, that we do not need to adopt P1. This clears the way for an alternative defence of emotional ambivalence: we can adopt P2. As we have seen, P2 implies that Orson's ambivalent evaluations$_i$ are not, in fact, inconsistent with each other. Hence there is no reason to suppose that his ambivalent response is irrational; nor do we need to suppose that it is partly misplaced. My own view is that this is the right verdict. Indeed, this is one reason I favour P2. I have a second, teleosemantic reason too. It seems implausible that our emotional evaluations$_i$ normally carry information about how a situation is likely to impact on our likes overall. Given that they are narrowly based, and often rather swift, assessments of the situation, P1 seems too demanding.

It is worth remembering, though, that P2 applies only to *personal* emotional responses. It remains possible that there are other cases of ambivalence – cases involving moral emotions, say – that do involve some kind of error. Try to imagine, for example, that Orson both (morally) admires Penny's intervention and regards it with indignation. When I try to imagine this scenario, I tend to suppose *either* that Orson admires and is indignant about different things (perhaps he admires Penny's kindness, but is indignant about her high-handedness); *or* that he is vacillating between two evaluations₁ of her behaviour. I find it difficult to imagine that he both admires and is indignant *about the same thing at the same time* – not without supposing that his evaluations₁ are confused in some problematic way. It is possible, then, that moral ambivalence involves a kind of confusion that personal ambivalence does not.

Emotional Ambivalence and Action

I have suggested that – as far as personal responses are concerned – emotional ambivalence involves no irrationality. This, though, should prompt a question. If Orson's resentment and his gratitude both fit the situation, why think that his emotions are *ambivalent*? Where is the conflict?

The answer lies with the motivational component of Orson's emotional responses. There is another sense in which emotional evaluations₁ can be regarded as 'all-out' evaluations₁: they are, we might say, *motivationally* all-out. Very crudely, Orson's grateful evaluation₁ motivates him to reward Penny for her action, while his resentful evaluation₁ motivates him to punish her for it. These motivations do not cancel each other out; nor do they combine to motivate some more nuanced response. Rather, each motivates behaviour that is likely to undermine the behaviour motivated by the other: a sour 'thank you' is effective neither as an expression of gratitude nor as an act of revenge. The conflict in this case is a *practical* one.

This, though, raises a possible worry for friends of ambivalence. It might be objected that, even if these two evaluations₁ do not contradict each other, it is *practically* irrational for

Orson to harbour them both (Pugmire, 2005: 182). Greenspan (1980, 1988) rejects this view (see also Rorty, 2010). She rejects it because, as she points out, different situations can call for different kinds of behaviour: when Orson is with Penny, the appropriate thing for him to do is to thank her sincerely and unreservedly; but, when he thinks through the situation alone, he should also resolve to keep his financial affairs hidden from her in future. Hence, an ambivalent emotional response can motivate us to behave in ways that match the complexities of the situation.

That seems right. Indeed, it is possible to see the phenomenon of emotional ambivalence as providing a kind of corrective to a potentially negative feature of emotion. For, as we have seen, one effect of an emotional response is to narrow our focus of attention and, in some cases, to restrict the kinds of behavioural option that we are able to consider. An ambivalent emotional response, in contrast, might sometimes constitute a more balanced, open-minded response to our situation (cf. de Sousa, 1987: 187; Rorty, 2010).

It is worth noting, however, that this story presupposes that Orson is able to control or manage his emotional response to some extent. It may be, then, that emotional ambivalence can have positive value only if the subject's emotional responses are not very intense.[4] Conceding that, though, the conclusion to draw is not that emotional ambivalence is practically irrational, but that it presents a practical *challenge* to be overcome. Orson might manage his emotional response well or badly; but this is true of any emotional response (Greenspan, 1980: 239–41).

Summary

In Chapter 5, I argued that emotional evaluations; are not evaluative judgements, but that they are closer to perceptions in some respects. In this chapter, however, we have found some reasons to qualify that claim. In particular, I have argued that emotional evaluations; differ from perceptual experiences in that they answer to *grounds*; and that it is this that explains why we are sometimes ready to describe recalcitrant emotions as irrational. In offering this account, however, I have not found reasons to vindicate the judgement view. Grounds for emotion, I suggested, are not exactly analogous to reasons for belief; moreover, our emotional evaluations¡ and our evaluative judgements answer to rather different standards of evidence. We might regard emotional evaluations¡ as occupying a kind of midway position between perception and judgement.

I ended by considering the phenomenon of emotional ambivalence. I endorsed Greenspan's view that emotional ambivalence is not always irrational, but I offered a different explanation for why this should be. Ambivalent emotions, I suggested, need not present contradictory assessments of the situation; rather the conflict between them is a practical one. But this practical conflict need not be paralysing or damaging. Indeed, there are reasons to value emotional ambivalence.

Further Reading

Conflict between emotion and judgement and the authority of emotion are discussed by Helm (2001: Chap. 5); Döring (2009, 2010). Discussions of the rationality of emotional recalcitrance include Roberts (2003: 91–3); Brady (2007, 2009); Tappolet (2012). Goldie (2005) provides an interesting discussion of the epistemic dangers of emotion; but for more positive views, see de Sousa (1987: 190–6); Morton (2010); Brady (2013). For Greenspan's views on the standards of evidence applicable to emotion, see Greenspan (1988: Chap. 4). For some discussions of emotional ambivalence see Greenspan (1980, 1988: Chap. 5); Pugmire (2005: Chap. 7); Tappolet (2005); Rorty (2010).

7
The Manipulation of Emotion

Introduction

In preceding chapters, we have considered some different ways in which emotional responses can be evaluated. A sad response *fits the situation*, I have suggested, when the subject has suffered a personally significant loss, and when their response is proportional to the significance of their loss. An emotional response is *well grounded* when it is justified by what the subject's believes or perceives to be the case. But there are other ways in which emotional responses can be evaluated: we might ask, for example, whether a particular emotional response is beneficial, or morally admirable, or charming.

In this final chapter, I would like to consider two other ways in which emotional responses can be assessed. First, I shall consider what it means to describe an emotional response as inauthentic or false. Secondly, I shall explore what it means to describe an emotional response as sentimental. In doing this, I shall explore how these notions relate to other ways of assessing emotional responses – as fitting or rational, say. Moreover, as we shall see, both these phenomena rest, in whole or in part, on our ability to deliberately *control* our emotional responses. Hence, they raise questions not only about the rationality of this kind of behaviour, but about its moral value too. Is our capacity to manipulate these kinds of emotional response always to be regretted?

Emotion and Authenticity

Varieties of Inauthenticity

A funeral cortège makes its way down a city street. The pavements are lined with solemn people: many are clutching flowers or banners; some are weeping. This, we can infer, is the funeral of someone who was well known and widely loved – a respected public figure, perhaps, or a celebrity who has died tragically young. For many of those present, the grief is real and sustained. This is true, in particular, of the family and friends of the deceased. It is true, too, of many people in the crowd: for them, the deceased was a significant figure – someone whom they admired or treasured. For some of the mourners, though, the death does not have this kind of significance: for them, the person who has died was, at most, an occasional source of entertaining news stories. They have not come to the funeral out of concern for the deceased or for the grieving family. Rather, they are motivated by a desire to claim a place in a poignant and momentous event. They too are clutching flowers and weeping; they too feel very sad.

What I tried to do in the last paragraph was to describe an emotional response that might be described as *false* or *inauthentic*. In recent years, there has been some debate about the extent to which the funerals of public figures have prompted displays of inauthentic grief. I am not going to take a view on this here. Still, it is hard to believe that this *never* happens at such events. It may happen at private funerals too. Nor is it hard to come up with other examples of inauthentic emotion. Devoted football supporters sometimes mutter darkly about 'fair-weather fans' – people who are triumphant when their team is victorious but show no interest in football at any other time. Again, someone might work themselves up into a lather about a colleague's behaviour, not because it really bothers them, but because they are spoiling for a fight.

In all these cases, it is natural to think of the subject's emotional response as *manufactured* or *fabricated* in some sense: it occurs, in part, because the subject wants it to occur.

Moreover, in all these cases, the subjects' motivations are essentially self-serving: the inauthentic mourners want to associate themselves with a momentous event; the fair-weather fans want the pleasure of lording it over rival supporters. Again, in all these cases, there seems to be an element of fantasy and self-deception: in each case, the subject would strongly resist the suggestion that their response is fabricated. We might call these cases of *self-deceptive manufacture*. When theorists of emotion discuss inauthentic emotion, they often have this kind of case in mind.

Plausibly, though, there are other kinds of inauthentic emotion. Suppose that Quinn, a teacher, is about to meet a group of children who will shortly be joining his school. He knows that some of the children will be feeling shy, and that it is important that he should look happy and enthusiastic. Unfortunately, he has recently split up with his girlfriend and is not in a cheerful mood. However, he remembers William James's advice that people can make themselves feel happier simply by straightening up and assuming a bright expression (James, 1890: 462–6). He follows this advice and finds that it works. Quinn's emotional response, then, is manufactured. In this case, though, no fantasy or self-deception is involved. We might call this a case of *clear-sighted manufacture*.

Finally, consider a case of emotional contagion. Imagine that you have entered a room in which people are enjoying themselves and laughing loudly over some joke that you did not hear. Perhaps when you entered the room you were feeling gloomy. But the atmosphere of jollity produces a sudden feeling of happiness. On another day, perhaps, you might have accepted this sudden change of tone: you might have evaluated the situation as joyful, and responded joyfully. On this occasion, though, your response strikes you as alien and strained. Arguably, this too is a case of inauthentic emotion: you resist your response precisely *because* it seems false. In this case, though, the response is not manufactured by the subject, but imposed from outside.

I have described three different cases in which a person's emotional response might be described as inauthentic. We might wonder whether these cases have something in common. I want to suggest that they do. I shall start by exploring some existing accounts of inauthentic emotion.

Accounting for Inauthenticity

Before I begin, it is worth noting a point of terminology. The word 'inauthentic' can be used in two senses. In one sense, it means 'fake'. To say that Quinn's happiness is inauthentic, in this sense, is to imply that it is not really happiness, just as a fake diamond is not really a diamond. Used in another sense, the term does not imply that his happiness is fake but, rather, that it is not a true or honest reflection of *himself*. Many theorists understand the term in the first sense (e.g. Dilman, 1989; Pugmire, 1994; Milligan, 2008). In contrast, I see no need to deny that Quinn is really happy or that the inauthentic mourners are really sad. Hence, I shall use the term purely in the second sense.

I shall begin by considering discussions by David Hamlyn (1989) and İlham Dilman (1989). Although they disagree on certain details, these theorists agree that an inauthentic emotion is one that has been manufactured by the subject: it is one that the subject wants to have and has somehow brought about in themselves. Moreover, both Hamlyn and Dilman emphasize the role of fantasy and self-deception in cases of inauthentic emotion. Their accounts, then, do a good job of characterizing cases of self-deceptive manufacture. However, they do not seem to cover cases of emotional contagion, or even cases of clear-sighted manufacture. We might wonder whether we can develop a more general account – one that will capture all these cases.

Like Hamlyn and Dilman, David Pugmire (1994) emphasizes the role of fantasy and self-deception in cases of inauthentic emotion. However, he adds a further claim. Pugmire is not committed to the view that emotional evaluations; are themselves beliefs. Nevertheless, he holds that, for some types of emotion, to describe an emotional response as authentic is to imply that it is ultimately rooted in the subject's evaluative beliefs about the situation. On his view, then, to describe someone's sorrow as inauthentic is to imply that they do not really believe that they have suffered a significant personal loss; or, at least, that their feelings cannot be traced back to this belief. An inauthentic emotional response, he suggests is one that has its roots in fantasy, rather than belief (see also Dilman, 1989: 288–9).

This suggestion allows Pugmire to account for a wider range of cases than Hamlyn or Dilman. Consider, first, the case of emotional contagion. In this case, as we have seen, it is perfectly possible that you believe that the occasion calls for joy. Still your emotional response does not *originate* in this belief; rather, it is triggered by the behaviour of the people around you. Similarly, Quinn may well believe that the arrival of a new batch of pupils is something to celebrate; again, though, his happy response is not rooted in this belief but, rather, in his belief that he owes it to his pupils to look happy to see them.

However, it is not clear that Pugmire has given the right account of self-deceptive manufacture. Consider again the case of the inauthentic mourners: on Pugmire's account, we need to suppose that their grief is not rooted in the belief that they have suffered a significant loss; at most, they have convinced themselves that they believe this (Pugmire, 1994: 115–16). In contrast, it seems to me to be quite possible that they *do* believe this: certainly, if the second form of self-deception is possible, it is unclear why the first should not be possible too. Moreover, if they have managed to convince themselves that they have suffered a genuine loss, this does not seem enough to ensure that their sorrow is authentic after all.

Arguably, too, Pugmire's account is too strong. Suppose, for example, that an old friend drops by unannounced, and I react with immediate joy, before I have had a chance to form a judgement. In this case, my emotional reaction is not rooted in my evaluative judgement; rather, it is one step ahead of it. Nevertheless, this seems to be a case of wholly authentic emotion – a spontaneous and heartfelt response to seeing my friend. For these reasons, then, I am not convinced that Pugmire has found the right way to characterize inauthentic emotion.

There is one final suggestion to consider. In a discussion of shame, Gabriele Taylor suggests that shame will be false if fails to reflect the subject's values. When this is not the case, she suggests, the emotional response is at odds with the subject's 'genuine self' (Taylor, 1985: 83, 140). At first glance, Taylor's account looks similar to Pugmire's; but the two accounts are not identical. While Pugmire appeals to the subject's evaluative judgement about their situation, Taylor appeals to the values or standards to which they are committed in the longer term. These two things can come apart: someone might be bullied or indoctrinated into believing that they have done something wrong on a particular occasion, even though this is at odds with their established values. Moreover, they might feel shame as a result. For Taylor, this would be an example of inauthentic shame. As a result, Taylor is able to avoid at least one of the objections that I made to Pugmire's account: my joyful reaction on seeing my friend might reflect my values, even if it is not rooted in an evaluative belief that my friend's arrival is a joyous event.

In the case of moral emotional responses, I think that Taylor's suggestion looks plausible. Unfortunately, though, it does not seem possible to carry it over to cases involving personal emotional responses. Consider the following case. Rachel is sincerely opposed to violence – including the war that her own county is currently waging abroad. Nevertheless, as she listens to the news reports describing the rout of the enemy, she realizes that she is feeling elated and triumphant. Her emotional response, she may rightly insist, does not reflect her values; indeed, she may well find her feelings disturbing or shameful. On the face of it, though, her feelings are not inauthentic. Plausibly, this is precisely *why* she finds them so unsettling: her feelings are not alien forces that are assailing her from outside; rather, they are telling her something about herself.

For this reason, then, I do not think that we can simply transfer Taylor's account to cases involving personal emotional responses. Nevertheless, it is not hard to see how we might develop an *analogous* account – one that draws on the likes-based account that I described in Chapter 6. In the next section, I shall develop this suggestion.

A Likes-Based Account of Inauthenticity

There is one aspect of Pugmire's account that I would like to endorse. This is the idea that authenticity has something to do with the *provenance* of the subject's response (see also

Milligan, 2008). This seems right. The challenge, though, is to say what kind of provenance an authentic response must have. I am going to suggest that, in the case of personal emotions, an authentic response is one that is rooted in the subject's likes and dislikes – or, at least, in an honest (non-self-deceptive) conception of their likes. If Rachel's sense of triumph is authentic, on this account, it is because it is rooted in her likes. Her likes, as much as her values, help to constitute her genuine self (cf. Baier, 1990; Haybron, 2008: 177–92).

'Rooted in' is stronger than 'accords with'. It is possible to imagine someone who is grieving for someone whom they genuinely loved whose sorrow is, nonetheless, manufactured. This might happen, for example, because they are still too numbed by shock to grieve authentically, but feel some kind of pressure to respond emotionally to the death. In this case, their grief accords with their love; but it is not rooted in it. Its causal origins are not of the right kind. Hence, their grief fits the situation, but it is not authentic.

None of the cases of inauthentic emotion that I have described meet this criterion. The inauthentic mourners feel sad not because they loved the person who has died, but because they are fantasizing that this is the case. Quinn feels happy not because the meeting with his new pupils has positive personal significance for him (even though it does), but because he has made an effort to manufacture a joyful response. In the case of emotional contagion, too, the subject's happiness is not explained by the personal significance that the situation has for them: it is simply triggered by the behaviour of the people around them.

Emotional responses that are inauthentic, on this account, will often be misplaced. As we have seen, though, this need not always be so: Quinn has good cause to feel happy about meeting his pupils. His response is inauthentic not because it fails to fit the situation, but because it has not been produced in the right way. Conversely, to say that an emotional response is misplaced need not imply that it is inauthentic. Suppose, for example, that a mother is overjoyed because her son has told her (falsely) that he has won a prize at school. Her joy is misplaced, but it may be authentic all the same.

Is there something *morally* objectionable about inauthentic emotion, understood in this way? Certainly, the behaviour of the inauthentic mourners appears to be morally objection-able: they have come to the funeral not out of genuine concern for the deceased or for the bereaved, but out of a desire to claim a place in the event. They are exploiting the situation for their own gratification, and in doing this, they are failing to pay proper regard to the seriousness of the occasion and the genuine distress of others present. To this extent, their behaviour is heartless and disrespectful, though they may not be in a position to recognize that this is so.

But there is no reason to suppose that all the cases that I have considered here are morally problematic. In cases of emotional contagion, for example, the subject does not appear to have done anything for which they could be criti-cized. (Indeed, they have not *done* anything at all.) Again, there seems very little to object to in Quinn's efforts to feel more enthusiastic about meeting his new pupils: he is not deceiving himself; nor is he deceiving his pupils about his character or motivations: he is at most disguising his mood.

Sentimentality

Two Views of Sentimentality

Sara is watching a news report describing a popular uprising against an unpleasant dictator. She wells up with compassion for the refugees fleeing from the conflict; she is stirred by admiration for the rebels fighting in the noble cause. She imagines herself bravely standing beside them at the barri-cades, tenderly caring for the wounded and indignantly upbraiding the tyrant. But she does nothing to try to help the refugees or the rebel cause; she does not even try to find out anything more about the rights or wrongs of the situation. Her response, we might think, is *sentimental*.

Sara's response to the news report is, I take it, not an unusual one. Noble freedom fighters, damsels in distress, cute children and animals are among the many stock objects of sentimental emotion. Theorists of emotion, though, have dis-agreed quite sharply about how to characterize and evaluate sentimental emotion. I shall start by considering two strongly opposed positions. These are the views of Anthony Savile (1982) and Robert Solomon (2004).

Sentimentality, writes Savile, is 'always open to criticism. There is always something wrong with it' (Savile, 1982: 237). A sentimental response is objectionable, Savile argues, because it is grounded in a *misrepresentation* of its object. Moreover, he suggests, sentimentality involves a particular kind of misrepresentation: '[W]hat distinguishes the sentimental fantasy…is its tendency to idealize its objects, to present them as pure, noble, heroic, vulnerable, innocent, etc.' (Savile, 1982: 241). Finally, he argues, the sentimental subject has a particular kind of motivation for engaging in this fantasy: a desire for gratification or reassurance. It is not hard to see how Savile might apply this account to Sara's case: Sara, he might suggest, has misrepresented the rebel cause, by exaggerating the nobility and heroism of the rebel fighters. She has done this because it enables her to enjoy pleasant feelings of admiration or indignation; or perhaps to enjoy an image of herself as someone who is caring and politically engaged. After all, as Savile wryly comments, it is far easier to construct an image of oneself as a caring person than to actually *be* such a person (Savile, 1982: 239).

Savile, then, takes a wholly negative view of sentimentality. Moreover, he is not alone in doing this. Compare, for example, what Mark Jefferson has to say:

> The qualities that sentimentality imposes on its objects are the qualities of innocence. But this almost inevitably involves a gross simplification of the nature of the object. And it is a simplification of an overtly moral significance. The simplistic appraisal necessary to sentimentality is also a direct impairment to the moral vision taken of its objects. (Jefferson, 1983: 527)

Jefferson, then, agrees with Savile that a sentimental emotional response almost always involves misrepresentation. He agrees too that this implies that sentimentality is almost always objectionable. Sentimentality, he suggests, involves not only misrepresentation but also a *moral* failing on the part of the subject – an impairment of the subject's moral vision (cf. Tanner, 1976; Kupfer, 1996; Pugmire, 2005).

However, not all philosophers have taken such a dim view of sentimentality. Solomon (2004), in particular, has written rousingly in its defence. It is significant, though, that his definition of sentimentality is much broader than the descriptions offered by Savile and Jefferson. Solomon takes sentimentality to involve certain types of emotional response – feelings of tenderness and compassion. These are, he suggests, the kinds of feelings elicited by small, innocent and vulnerable things. As he points out, this need not involve misrepresentation: babies and puppies *are* small, innocent and vulnerable. Moreover, Solomon argues, there is nothing wrong with enjoying the feelings of tenderness and warmth elicited by small, vulnerable things. He does not deny that *some* sentimental responses involve misrepresentation or harmful self-indulgence: his target is the blanket (or near blanket) condemnation offered by philosophers such as Savile and Jefferson.[1]

It is not hard to see, then, how the disagreement between Savile and Solomon arises. Savile starts from a very narrow definition of sentimentality: for him, a sentimental emotional response is one that involves a motivated idealization of its object. In contrast, Solomon begins from a much broader definition: for him, sentimentality is simply a matter of responding to a situation with warm and tender feelings, whether this involves misrepresentation or not. It is not obvious how the issue of definition is to be settled: as Martha Eaton (1989) has pointed out, the terms 'sentimentality' and 'sentimental' do not have a clearly defined meaning in everyday talk. Moreover, while Solomon's use of the term seems closer to everyday usage, it is not obvious that Savile's primary aim is to capture the ordinary meaning of the word. Rather, he might be interpreted as trying to delineate a particular kind of emotional phenomenon that he takes to be philosophically interesting and morally important. To an extent, then, the participants in this debate are in danger of simply talking past each other.

Nevertheless, I think that there is scope for meaningful disagreement about the nature of sentimentality. I accept that Solomon is right to point out that the everyday use of the term 'sentimental' is much broader than Savile and Jefferson allow. Nevertheless, I do think that Savile has identified an emotional phenomenon – motivated idealization – that is interesting and important. Moreover, it is this notion that seems to be at stake in much of the philosophical debate about sentimentality. In what follows, I shall go on referring to this phenomenon as 'sentimentality', though I concede that, in doing so, I am using the term in a rather specialized sense.

Moreover, I want to suggest that Savile's characterization of this emotional phenomenon can be improved – in two ways. First, I shall argue that sentimentality, even in this narrow sense, does not necessarily involve a *misrepresentation* of the object. Secondly, I shall argue that it is not always motivated by a self-indulgent desire for gratification or reassurance. Once we see this, I shall conclude, there is no need to insist that sentimentality, in this narrow sense, is always open to criticism. (My account, though, concerns only sentimental emotional *responses*: it is a further question whether sentimental representations in literature or art are always to be condemned.)

Sentimentality and Idealization

Consider, again, Sara's feelings of compassion for the refugees fleeing from the fighting. In what sense can she be said to have idealized the situation? On Savile's account, to describe Sara's compassion as sentimental is to imply that it somehow *misrepresents* the suffering or vulnerability of the refugees. It is not clear, though, that this is true: the refugees may well be suffering and vulnerable.

This is not to deny that there are *some* cases of sentimentality in which the subject's representation of the object is quite false: an ageing party worker who once served a murderous tyrant might now fondly remember her leader as a wise and benevolent man who only wanted the best for his people. In this case, the subject's fond feelings are not only sentimental but also wholly misplaced. In other cases, the sentimental subject may well *exaggerate* the qualities of courage, innocence, and so on, that they are ascribing to the object of their emotional response. In yet other cases, they may *underplay* the emotional significance of the situation: Sara, we might suspect, has only a limited appreciation of how miserable the refugees really are. It may be true, then, that sentimental emotional responses are often misplaced. But misrepresentation does not seem to be *essential* to sentimentality: Sara's response might be sentimental, even though, if only by luck, she has pitched it right.

Ira Newman (2002) describes a second sense in which a sentimental response might be thought to idealize the situation. A sentimental response, he suggests, is one that is highly *selective*: Sara, perhaps, is focusing tenderly on the suffering and vulnerability of the refugees, while skating over the distressing details of the situation: the filth in the camps, the dying children; the fights over water and food. She seems to be overlooking, too, her own relation to the situation – in particular, the fact that she could, and should, do something to help.

There seems to be something right in Newman's suggestion. Still, it is too strong as it stands. As we have seen, *all* emotional responses are selective in the sense that they are concerned with a particular aspect of the situation. Consider, for example, the compassion of an aid worker, Theo, who is trying to help the refugees. Theo may well be focusing on the needs of the refugees, while ignoring the dirt and the danger. If so, his emotional response is a selective one, but that is not to say that it is sentimental. Sentimentality, then, involves a particular *kind* of selectivity. But what kind? Pugmire, I want to suggest, offers a convincing answer to this question. A sentimental response, he suggests, is selective in the sense that it is *shallow* (Pugmire, 2005: 129).

To understand this suggestion, it helps to start from Pugmire's account of emotional profundity or depth (Pugmire, 2005: 30–70). His account is complex and nuanced, but there are two points that are particularly relevant here. A profound emotional response, Pugmire suggests, is one that that touches on the subject's values and concerns in many different ways or one that involves a wide range of further motivations and emotional dispositions. Moreover, he argues, this complexity in the subject's emotional response must reflect a corresponding complexity in its object. If the subject has credited the object with all kinds of significant features that it does not actually possess, their emotional response cannot be said to be profound.

Putting these two points together, they imply, I think, that profundity in emotion is partly *epistemic*: a profound emotional response is one that is grounded in a complex *understanding* of the emotional significance of the event. To describe Theo's compassion as profound, for example, is to imply that it reflects a rich appreciation of the many different ways in which the refugees' situation is miserable and the many different ways in which the situation calls for his help. A profound emotional response may nonetheless be *selective*: Theo may well be focused purely on the plight of the refugees, and not, say, on the injustice of their situation. What matters, though, is that his appreciation of the refugees' plight is not itself selective, but sensitive and wide-ranging.

Conversely, a shallow emotional response is one that rests on a relatively cursory or superficial grasp of the situation. This certainly seems true in Sara's case. As she tenderly contemplates the refugees' plight, she does not give them much thought. She sees them as victims of an awful situation, uprooted and vulnerable; but she goes no further than that. If she were to investigate their situation more deeply, she might well begin to uncover details that elicit not just gentle, tender feelings, but real horror, anger or shame – feelings that might motivate her to act. But her interest in the situation does not extend this far.

I agree with Pugmire, then, in holding that a sentimental response idealizes the situation in the sense that it represents it in only a very superficial way. Indeed, this seems true even in cases of sentimentality that involve misrepresentation. Recall the case of the ageing party worker who remembers her dead leader as a wise and kindly man who only wanted the best for his people. Given that he was, in fact, a murderous tyrant, this description is false. But it is also superficial and trite. Moreover, it is the superficiality, rather than the falsity, that marks her response as sentimental. If her admiration were grounded in a rich and detailed narrative about her leader's (fictional) virtues and achievements, her admiration would be misplaced, even deluded; but it would not be sentimental.

Still, not all shallow responses are sentimental. Emotional responses are often shallow simply because we do not have time to appreciate the emotional significance of the situation. I hear about a civil war far away, pause for a moment to think of the casualties and the refugees, and then move on. A shallow, cursory response of this kind seems to be quite the opposite of a sentimental one: a sentimental response is one that *dwells* on its object, albeit in a shallow way. To understand this point, we need to pay attention to the second aspect of Savile's account: the subject's motivation.

Sentimentality and Motivation

According to Savile, sentimentality is, in part a matter of motivation: sentimental subjects are *motivated* to idealize the situation. This looks like a plausible way to explain the difference between a merely cursory emotional response and a sentimental one. A sentimental response is shallow not because the subject is distracted or short of time, but because they are motivated to keep to the shallows (cf. Pugmire, 2005: 128).

Not all cases of motivated shallowness are cases of sentimentality. Imagine the case of a police officer attending a distressing scene after a road accident. She knows that, to do her job, she needs to keep her emotions in check: she makes a deliberate effort not to dwell on the victims' situation or to think about their families. In this respect, then, her response is more like Sara's than Theo's. Nevertheless, this case differs from Sara's in a crucial respect. For Sara, the emotional response is itself the object of her desire: she manipulates her emotions with a view to creating a response of the right kind. The police officer's goal, in contrast, is not to conjure up a shallow emotional response but, rather, to avoid a profound one. It would be all the same to her if she did not respond emotionally at all.

Is sentimentality always motivated? Certainly, it is not always entirely the subject's own work. Sentimentality can be elicited by others: mawkish films, heart-warming news reports and syrupy greetings cards are designed to prompt a shallow, reassuring response. Still, in these cases, the subject is often in a position to recognize that their feelings are being manipulated in this way; and they may well be allowing this to happen. Moreover, where this is not the case, it is not clear that their emotional response should be described as sentimental. When an adult and a small child are weeping together in front of a mawkish film, the adult's emotional response may well be sentimental. But it seems odd to describe the child's feelings in this way: the child is not *complicit* in the process in the way that the adult is.

Does sentimentality imply a particular *kind* of motivation? According to Savile, as we have seen, it implies a desire for gratification or reassurance. The sentimental subject, he implies, is more interested in their emotional response than in the situation itself. They are enjoying feeling tender, or admiring or indignant; or perhaps they are enjoying thinking of themselves as a caring and sensitive person. This certainly looks like a plausible way to describe Sara's case. I would like to suggest, though, that the motivation underlying a sentimental response might not always be as self-indulgent as Savile implies.

Suppose, for example, that two brothers are remembering their father, who died some time ago. Their father, I shall suppose, was a rather complex person: at times, he was generous and funny; but he could also be domineering and unkind. Moreover, these aspects of his character were linked: his generosity could sometimes be controlling, his sense of humour somewhat spiteful. The brothers are reminiscing about a childhood picnic – remembering the huge hamper their father had produced from the car boot and the funny song he made up about a teacher whom they both disliked. Neither mentions that, on the return journey, he lost his temper and ordered them out of the car. They are focusing on the golden hours earlier in the day; and they are not analysing those very closely, either. Their recollection of the picnic, then, is somewhat sentimental. It is possible, though, that in recalling the event in this way, they are not indulging *themselves*. Rather, they may be indulging *him*. It may be, after all, that they are both well aware of his flaws and the damage they caused. But they are not thinking about this today. Perhaps they feel that they owe it to him to remember him sometimes in soft focus. Perhaps they do this out of kindness, or even out of love.

Evaluating Sentimentality

Sentimentality, Savile claims, is always open to criticism. This is, in part, because he holds that a sentimental response always involves a misrepresentation of its object, and so will always be misplaced. In contrast, I have argued that this is not the case.

As we have seen, however, there is a second charge that might be laid against sentimentality – that it is always *morally* objectionable. In particular, it might be suggested that there is something dishonest or cowardly about the sentimental subject's refusal to look too deeply at the situation. Why, though, should this be? The problem cannot be simply that sentimental responses are deliberately shallow: as we have seen, a police officer might make a deliberate effort not to engage too deeply with the situation they are trying to repair; and there seems to be nothing problematic about that.

Alternatively, it might be suggested that it is the *nature* of the subject's motivation that is morally objectionable. Savile suggests that sentimentality is always motivated by a self-indulgent desire for gratification or reassurance. But even if this were so, it would not follow that sentimentality is always open to moral criticism: as Solomon (2004) points out, it is not always wrong to indulge in something just because it is pleasant. There seems no harm, for example, in allowing oneself a certain amount of cooing on being shown a neighbour's new baby or in enjoying sentimental reminiscences at a family celebration. Moreover, I have suggested that sentimentality need not always be self-indulgent. Nor does it seem to be incompatible with profound emotion: deep and honest love does not preclude the occasional sentimental moment.

This is not to deny, though, that sentimentality can *sometimes* be morally problematic. There are at least three reasons for this. In some cases, sentimentality seems to involve a kind of laziness: one is content to sigh pensively at the photograph of the starving child, rather than responding to more effect. The result is a missed opportunity. Secondly, as Savile points out, sentimentality is sometimes part of a self-deceptive strategy: it is just *because* one is convinced of one's own sensitivity and compassion that one fails to look any deeper. In cases like this, the sentimental response is not simply lazy but dishonest and self-serving. Finally, even cases in which sentimentality is aimed only at the pleasure of the emotional response itself – the warm glow – there is a risk that this pleasure is sought at the expense of its object: the object is treated not as a genuine object of concern, but simply as a means to the subject's pleasure. In cases of this kind, the problem with sentimentality is that – like the sorrow of the inauthentic mourners – it is exploitative and disrespectful.

I have suggested, then, that sentimentality is not always innocent or sociable – it can be lazy, self-serving or exploitative. But there is nothing *intrinsically* wrong with sentimentality; indeed, in some situations, a little motivated idealization may be just what is required.

Summary

The emotional phenomena discussed in this chapter arise from our capacity to control our emotional responses. The possibility of inauthentic emotion arises, in part, because we have the capacity to *manufacture* an emotional response – for example, by fantasizing or by exploiting feedback mechanisms. In the case of personal emotional responses, a response that originates in this way will be inauthentic not because it does not reflect the subject's beliefs or values (perhaps it does), but because it is not rooted in their likes. For our likes, no less than our values, are aspects of our selves. Sentimentality, in contrast, only rarely involves wholesale manufacture. More usually, it is achieved through the control of attention, allowing the subject to ensure that their response is safely or gratifyingly shallow. Hence, while an inauthentic response is one that fails to reflect its *subject*, a sentimental response is one that fails to do justice to its *object*.

Nevertheless, these phenomena need not involve misrepresentation or irrationality. An inauthentic response is not rooted in the subject's likes, but it may nevertheless *accord* with their likes; and so it may fit the situation. A sentimental response is shallow, but there is no general rational requirement that our emotional responses should be profound:

indeed, an emotional response may need to be shallow in order to do its job. Nevertheless, like other theorists, I take it that our capacity to manipulate our emotional responses does pose moral dangers: inauthentic and sentimental responses can be dishonest and exploitative. However, the picture is not a simple one: it is not hard to find cases in which the subject's motivations are innocent or even kind. Like other aspects of emotion, inauthenticity and sentimentality are complex and diverse phenomena.

Further Reading

For some discussions of inauthentic emotion, see Dilman (1989); Hamlyn (1989); Pugmire (1994); Milligan (2008). For a discussion of the authenticity, specifically, of happiness, see Haybron (2008: Chap. 9). Discussions of the nature and value of sentimentality abound; but see especially Tanner (1976); Savile (1982); Jefferson (1983); Kupfer (1996); Newman (2002); Solomon (2004); Pugmire (2005: Chap. 5). (Pugmire's account of profundity in emotion can be found in Pugmire, 2005: Chap. 2.) For some discussions about the very concept of sentimentality, and philosophers' attitudes to it, see Eaton (1989); Knight (1999).

Conclusion

Emotional responses, I suggested in Chapter 1, are both complex and diverse: they have many different components; they come in different shapes and sizes. This sets a challenge for theorists of emotion: how can we make sense of such a complicated phenomenon? In Chapter 2, we considered some different ways in which theorists of emotion have responded to this challenge.

In Chapter 3, I proposed a particular approach to the problem – one that emphasizes a further characteristic of emotion: its coherence. Emotional responses do not appear to be just random collections of symptoms: they *make sense*, seen as co-ordinated responses to particular kinds of situation. As I explained in that chapter, there are various ways in which the coherence of emotion might be explained. In this book, however, I have emphasized one particular approach – an approach that foregrounds the functional properties of emotion. I have appealed to this approach in a number of ways throughout my discussion.

What kind of picture has emerged? It is one in which no particular emotional phenomenon stands out as *the* crucial component of an emotional response. Hence in Chapter 4, I resisted the demand to state what I take an instance of emotion to be: I argued that we might do better to offer an account of emotional *phenomena*, in all their diversity. I suggested that it is by considering how emotional responses fit together and what they function to do that we can best understand how they differ from other psychological phenomena. I emphasized, too, that in explaining the phenomenal character of emotion and its intentional properties, we need to take account of the whole emotional response.

Still, in the second half of the book, I focused on a particular emotional phenomenon – the emotional evaluations$_i$ that initiate our emotional responses. These states, I argued, are not evaluative judgements; nor, I think, are they best understood as perceptions. Nevertheless, they are similar to perceptions in some significant ways: in particular, they are not produced by conscious deliberation, nor are they directly responsive to reasoning, as judgements are. Unlike perceptions, though, they often depend on our existing perceptions and beliefs about the situation, and for this reason, it makes sense to ask whether they are well or poorly grounded.

Emotional evaluations$_i$, I argued, have two functions: to trigger an emotional response when an emotionally significant situation has arisen and to motivate behaviour that will help to deal with the situation. What constitutes emotional significance will depend on what kind of emotional response is involved. I suggested (albeit tentatively) that the evaluations$_i$ that trigger many of our personal emotional responses are concerned with situations in which our likes *and* dislikes are at stake. It follows, then, that these personal emotional responses will fit the situation only when they properly reflect our likes; they will be authentic only when they are rooted in our likes. Our likes and dislikes are not merely passing fancies: they are fundamental concerns of ours, which reflect our needs as biological and social beings, and which are shaped by our experience of the world. Hence, our personal emotional evaluations$_i$, have something *important* to tell us, something that risks being overlooked when they are misplaced or merely sentimental. Still, they do not represent *everything* that matters to us. We might see them, instead, as somewhat vociferous advocates for a particular subset of our concerns. We would do well to take them seriously, but they need not always have the final word.

Glossary

This glossary is not intended to act as a general philosophical dictionary, but just to capture the ways in which certain terms are used in this book.

Affective perception. On Döring's (2003, 2007) account, emotional evaluations₁ (q.v.) constitute a discrete class of perceptions, distinct from bodily feelings and external sense perceptions (q.v.), which she labels 'affective perceptions'. (See also *strong perception theory.*)

Coherence (of emotion). The term 'coherence' is used throughout the book to express the idea that complex emotional responses appear to be organized, co-ordinated responses, designed to deal with a particular kind of challenge or opportunity.

Complex process theory. Complex process theorists take an instance of emotion to be a complex response – for example, an emotional reaction or an emotional attitude.

Complexity (of emotion). The term 'complexity' is used throughout the book to express the idea that emotional responses involve many different components, including thoughts, feelings, desires, and so on.

Descriptive content. An intentional state (q.v.) has descriptive content if it represents a certain state of affairs as *being the case*. For example, beliefs and perceptions have descriptive content. (See also *directive content.*)

Directive content. An intentional state (q.v.) has directive content if it represents some goal to be achieved or some activity to be performed. For example, desires, wishes and intentions have directive content. (See also *descriptive content.*)

Dislike. A settled disposition to experience something as unpleasant or distressing. (See also *like.*)

Diversity (of emotion). The term 'diversity' is used throughout the book to express the idea that there are many different types of emotional response and that emotional responses come in a variety of shapes and sizes, including reactions, episodes and attitudes.

Embodied appraisal. On Prinz's (2004) account, an embodied appraisal is an intentional state (q.v.) that registers that certain changes are occurring in the subject's body but functions to signal that a particular kind of situation has arisen in the environment. An embodied appraisal is usually accompanied by a valence marker (q.v.). (See also *'judgement of the body'.*)

Emotional ambivalence. Emotional ambivalence occurs when a person's emotional response to a particular aspect of the situation involves two or more distinct types of emotional evaluation$_i$ (q.v.) and at least one of these evaluations$_i$ implies that this aspect of the situation has *positive* emotional significance (q.v.) for the subject, while at least one implies that it has *negative* emotional significance.

Emotional attitude. An enduring emotional response that has the potential to last a lifetime.

Emotional disposition. See *emotional susceptibility.*

Emotional episode. A sustained emotional response, which characteristically originates in an emotional reaction (q.v.), but which may involve thoughts, memories, images, reasoning about how to deal with the situation, actions and further emotional reactions. An emotional episode might last for minutes or extend over days, weeks or months.

Emotional evaluation$_i$. An intentional state (q.v.) that initiates an emotional response.

Emotional reaction. A brief emotional response, characteristically involving an evaluation, a switch of attention and various motivational, behavioural and physiological changes. An emotional reaction might fade after a few seconds or develop into an emotional episode (q.v.).

Emotional significance. An emotionally significant situation is one that merits an emotional response of a particular kind. For example, an emotionally significant loss is a loss that merits a sad response; an emotionally significant success is a success that merits a joyful response; and so on. (See also *personal significance.*)

Emotional susceptibility (or disposition). A propensity to react with a particular emotion in a certain kind of situation or in response to a particular person or object.

Evaluative judgement. A judgement (q.v.) that assigns a certain value (or disvalue) to something: for example, the judgement that piranhas are impressive or that rollercoasters are dangerous. (See also *non-evaluative judgement.*)

External sense perception. A perception of some object or feature in the subject's environment: for example, seeing an aubergine as purple or hearing a note as flat.

'Feeling towards'. On Goldie's (2000) account, a 'feeling towards' is an evaluation of the situation which is neither a judgement nor a perception, though it is like a perception in some ways. A 'feeling towards' has a phenomenal character (q.v.) but it is not a bodily feeling. (See also *weak perception theory.*)

Fit. An emotional evaluation$_i$ (q.v.) fits the situation when the situation is as the evaluation represents it to be. An evaluation$_i$ that does not fit the situation is misplaced.

Function. See *historical theory (of functions).*

Functional claim. The claim that one important way in which we can explain why emotional responses take the form that they do is by appealing to their functional properties.

Grounds. The considerations or evidence on which (for example) an emotional evaluation$_i$ (q.v.) is based.

Historical theory (of functions). The view that the function of a particular item, for example an artefact or a biological system, is determined by its history. On the account endorsed here, the function of a biological organ or system is the specific and direct contribution that organs or systems of that type have historically made to other organs and systems in the body, so explaining why this particular organ or system exists or is present. (See also *normally.*)

Inauthentic emotion. As the term is used here, to describe an emotional response as inauthentic is to imply that it is not a true reflection of the subject's self.

Intellectual emotional response. An emotional response that has to do with the subject's ability or need to understand something: for example, wonder at something never experienced before, or interest in a question that would be worth investigating. (See also *moral emotional response, personal emotional response.*)

Intentional content. The content of an intentional state (q.v.) is what it represents. (See also *descriptive content, directive content.*)

Intentional state. An intentional state is a state that stands for or represents something else: for example, an object, action or state of affairs. Beliefs, desires, perceptions and emotional evaluations are kinds of intentional state.

Intentional system. A system that produces intentional states (q.v.).

Judgement. As the term is used here, a judgement is the act of forming a belief. (See also *evaluative judgement, non-evaluative judgement.*)

'Judgement of the body'. On Solomon's (2003b) account the bodily feelings involved in an emotional response may well function to alert the subject that some emotionally significant situation has arisen. A 'judgement of the body' does not seem to be a judgement (q.v.) in the usual sense of the word. (See also *embodied appraisal.*)

Judgement view. The view that emotional evaluations; (q.v.) are judgements (q.v.).

Like. A settled disposition to experience something as pleasant or rewarding. (See also *dislike.*)

Moral emotional response. An emotional response that has to do with the moral features of the situation (as opposed to, say, the subject's own concerns). (See also *intellectual emotional response, personal emotional response.*)

Narrative structure. When Goldie (2000) suggests that emotions have a narrative structure, he is claiming that the way in which a particular instance of emotion develops is best understood against the background of the subject's experiences, beliefs and character.

Non-evaluative judgement. A judgement (q.v.) that assigns no particular value or disvalue to its object: for example, the judgement that piranhas eat meat or that rollercoasters are commonly found in theme parks. (See also *evaluative judgement.*)

Normally. The way in which a type of biological organ or system has historically succeeded in performing its function.

Objectless emotion. An emotional response that is not directed towards any particular object or situation.

Perception view. See *strong perception view, weak perception view.*

Personal emotional response. An emotional response that has to do with the subject's own concerns (as opposed to, say, the moral features of the situation). (See also *intellectual emotional response, moral emotional response.*)

Personal significance. A personally significant situation bears on the subject's concerns, so as to merit a personal emotional response (q.v.) of a particular kind. (See also *emotional significance.*)

Phenomenal character (or phenomenology). The way a particular experience feels, or what it is like to have it.

Recalcitrant emotion. A recalcitrant emotional response is one that conflicts with the subject's judgements about the situation, in the sense that, if the subject's judgements are true, their emotional response must be misplaced.

Sentimental emotion. The meaning of the term 'sentimental' is disputed. Here, I am particularly interested in Savile's (1982) suggestion that a sentimental response idealizes its object and is motivated.

Strong perception view. The view that emotional evaluations; (q.v.) are perceptions of some kind. (See also *affective perception, embodied appraisal, weak perception view.*)

Structural question. A question about why an emotional response takes the form that it does: for example, why it involves certain kinds of motivation or thought. Broadbrush structural questions concern types of emotional response; fine-grained structural questions concern individual responses.

Teleosemantic theory. A theory of intentional content (q.v.) that takes the content of an intentional state to depend on the function of the system that produced it and on the way in which the system normally (q.v.) works (e.g. the information that it normally carries).

Valence marker. On Prinz's (2004) account, a valence marker is a signal that accompanies an embodied appraisal (q.v.) and which tags the situation as good or bad.

Values. (When used to refer to a person's values.) Someone's settled beliefs about the kinds of thing that are worth respecting, promoting or pursuing.

Weak perception view. The view that emotional evaluations (q.v), though not literally perceptions, are like perceptions in some important ways. (See also *'feeling towards'*, *strong perception view*.)

Notes

Chapter 1   Introduction

1   For a defence of the claim that love is an emotional attitude, and not merely a complex emotional disposition, see Price (2012a).

Chapter 2   Four Theories of Emotion

1   The thesis is often referred to as the James–Lange theory of emotion, since, as James acknowledges, a similar view was advocated by the Danish theorist Carl Lange (1922 [1885]).
2   Prinz cites a study by Hohmann (1966) that seems to support James's thesis; and a study by Chwalisz et al. (1988) that seems to undermine it.
3   For a defence of this kind, see Whiting (2011).
4   Whether or not beliefs and judgements have a phenomenology is a matter of some controversy. For some discussions of this issue, see Bayne and Montague (2011).

Chapter 3   Emotion, Coherence and Function

1 See also Tooby and Cosmides (1990: 407–8); Lazarus (1991: 202); Johnson-Laird and Oatley (1992: 204–8); Griffiths (1997: Chap. 3).
2 For other examples of this kind of theory, see Millikan (1989); Neander (1991). For a fuller version of my own account, see Price (2001). For some opposing views, see Cummins (1975); Schlosser (1998); Hardcastle (1999).
3 Griffiths (1993) and Godfrey-Smith (1994) make a similar point.
4 For discussion, see Price (2001: 58–60).
5 For discussion of this issue, see Griffiths (1997: 71–4).
6 For an account of this kind, see Price (2012a).
7 For further discussion, see Price (2010).

Chapter 4   What Is an Emotion?

1 Indeed, there is at least one other possible strategy (the 'causal strategy') that I do not have space to consider here (for discussion, see Price, 2012b).
2 The suggestion that an emotion is an emotional evaluation has been endorsed by many theorists, including Roberts (1988), Nussbaum (2001) and Helm (2001).
3 Prinz (2004: 3–20) provides a helpful discussion of the territory.
4 Similarly, Joel Marks (1982) argues that an emotion is a combination of belief and desire.
5 For some objections to Goldie's emphasis on emotional attitudes, see Tappolet (2002).
6 Dread and relief also seem to lack a motivational component.
7 Not everyone agrees: see, for example, Ben Ze'ev (2000: 405–48).

Chapter 5   What Is an Emotional Evaluation?

1 Examples include de Sousa (1987); Roberts (1988, 2003); Montague (2009). Theorists who suggest that these intentional states are perceptions include Döring (2003, 2007); Prinz (2004); Deonna (2006); Tappolet (2012).

2 For some discussions, see the papers in Bayne and Montague (2011). The introduction to this collection provides a very helpful overview of the debate.
3 This is a point made by Patricia Greenspan (1988: 19).
4 Helm (2009: 249) might be read as endorsing this view.
5 This worry is voiced by Goldie (2009: 235–6); and by Deigh (2010: 36).
6 For another suggestion, see Deonna (2006).

Chapter 6 What Are Emotional Evaluations About?

1 For some objections to teleosemantic theories, see Fodor (1990); Sterelny (1990: 128–34).
2 For a more detailed discussion of this issue, albeit one that takes no account of the teleosemantic theory, see Price (2013).
3 See also Lyons (1980: 35); Roberts (2003: 141–8).
4 Arguably, Helm is offering an account of what it means for an emotional response to be *rational*, rather than fitting. As I read him, he is doing both these things.

Chapter 7 The Rationality of Emotion

1 In Brady (2009) he is concerned, not only with the perceptual theory, but a range of alternatives to the judgement theory; here, though, I am concerned only with his account as a possible addition to a perceptual theory.
2 For a detailed consideration of the epistemic dangers posed by emotion, see Goldie (2005).
3 For further discussion, see Marino (2010).
4 This point is made by both Greenspan (1980: 239; 1988: 116–17) and Pugmire (2005: 177).

Chapter 8 The Manipulation of Emotion

1 For another dissenting voice, see Knight (1999).

References

Allen, C. (2009) 'Teleological notions in biology', in *The Stanford Encyclopedia of Philosophy* (Winter Edition), ed. E. Zalta: http://plato.stanford.edu/archives/win2009/entries/teleology-biology/.

Aristotle (1985) *Nicomachean Ethics*, T. Irwin (trans.). Indianapolis, IN: Hackett.

Armon-Jones, C. (1986) 'The social functions of emotion', in R. Harré (ed.), *The Social Construction of Emotions*. Oxford: Blackwell: 57–82.

Averill, J. (1980) 'A constructivist view of emotion', in R. Plutchik and H. Kellerman (eds), *Emotion: Theory, Research and Experience, Vol. 1: Theories of Emotion*. New York: Academic Press: 305–39.

Baier, A. (1990) 'What emotions are about', *Philosophical Perspectives* 4: 1–29.

Baier, A. (2004) 'Feelings that matter', in R. Solomon (ed.), *Thinking about Feeling*. Oxford: Oxford University Press: 200–13.

Bayne, T. and Montague, M. (eds) (2011) *Cognitive Phenomenology*. Oxford: Oxford University Press.

Ben-Ze'ev, A. (2000) *The Subtlety of Emotions*. Cambridge, MA: MIT Press.

Brady, M. (2007) 'Recalcitrant emotions and visual illusions', *American Philosophical Quarterly* 44(3): 273–84.

Brady, M. (2009) 'The irrationality of recalcitrant emotions', *Philosophical Studies* 145(3): 413–30.

Brady, M. (2013) *Emotional Insight: The Epistemic Role of Emotional Experience*. Oxford: Oxford University Press.

Chwalisz, K., Diener, E. and Gallagher, D. (1988) 'Autonomic arousal feedback and emotional experience: evidence from the spinal cord injured', *Journal of Personality and Social Psychology* 54(5): 820–8.

Cowie, R. (2010) 'Forms of emotional colouring in everyday life', in P. Goldie (ed.), *The Oxford Handbook of Philosophy of Emotion*. Oxford: Oxford University Press: 63–94.

Cummins, R. (1975) 'Functional analysis', *Journal of Philosophy* 72: 741–65.

D'Arms, J. and Jacobson, D. (2003) 'The significance of recalcitrant emotion (or, anti-quasijudgmentalism)', in A. Hatzimoysis (ed.), *Philosophy and the Emotions*. Cambridge: Cambridge University Press: 113–45.

de Sousa, R. (1987) *The Rationality of Emotion*. Cambridge, MA: MIT Press.

de Sousa, R. (2014) 'Emotion', in *The Stanford Encyclopedia of Philosophy* (Spring Edition), ed. E. Zalta: http://plato.stanford.edu/archives/spr2014/entries/emotion/.

Deigh, J. (2010) 'Concepts of emotions in modern philosophy and psychology', in P. Goldie (ed.), *The Oxford Handbook of Emotion*. Oxford: Oxford University Press: 17–40.

DeLancey, C. (2002) *Passionate Engines: What Emotions Reveal About Mind and Artificial Intelligence*. Oxford: Oxford University Press.

Deonna, J. (2006) 'Emotion, perception and perspective', *Dialectica* 60(1): 29–46.

Deonna, J. and Teroni, F. (2012) *The Emotions: A Philosophical Introduction*. London: Routledge.

Dilman, İ. (1989) 'False emotions', *Proceedings of the Aristotelian Society* Supp. Vol. 63: 287–95.

Döring, S. (2003) 'Explaining action by emotion', *Philosophical Quarterly* 53(211): 214–30.

Döring, S. (2007) 'Seeing what to do: affective perception and rational motivation', *Dialectica* 61(3): 363–94.

Döring, S. (2009) 'The logic of emotional experience: non-inferentiality and the problem of conflict without contradiction', *Emotion Review* 1(3): 240–7.

Döring, S. (2010) 'Why be emotional?', in P. Goldie (ed.), *The Oxford Handbook of Philosophy of Emotion*. Oxford: Oxford University Press: 283–301.

Dretske, F. (1995) *Naturalizing the Mind*. Cambridge, MA: MIT Press.

Eaton, M. (1989) 'Laughing at the death of Little Nell: sentimental art and sentimental people', *American Philosophical Quarterly* 26(4): 269–82.

Ekman, P. (1992) 'An argument for basic emotions', *Cognition and Emotion* 6(3–4): 169–200.

Ekman, P. (1994a) 'All emotions are basic', in P. Ekman and R. Davidson (eds), *The Nature of Emotion*. Oxford: Oxford University Press: 15–19.

Ekman, P. (1994b) 'Moods, emotions and traits', in P. Ekman and R. Davidson (eds), *The Nature of Emotion*. Oxford: Oxford University Press: 56–8.

Fodor, J. (1990) *A Theory of Content and Other Essays*. Cambridge, MA: MIT Press.

Godfrey-Smith, P. (1994) 'A modern history theory of functions', *Noûs* 28(3): 344–62.

Goldie, P. (2000) *The Emotions: A Philosophical Exploration*. Oxford: Oxford University Press.

Goldie, P. (2002) 'Emotions, feelings and intentionality', *Phenomenology and the Cognitive Sciences* 1(3): 235–54.

Goldie, P. (2005) 'Imagination and the distorting power of emotion', *Journal of Consciousness Studies* 12(8–10):127–39.

Goldie, P. (2007) 'Emotion', *Philosophy Compass* 2(6): 928–38.

Goldie, P. (2009) 'Getting feelings into emotional experience in the right way', *Emotion Review* 1(3): 232–9.

Goldie P. (ed.) (2010) *The Oxford Handbook of Philosophy of Emotion*. Oxford: Oxford University Press.

Greenspan, P. (1980) 'A case of mixed feelings: ambivalence and the logic of emotion', in A. Rorty (ed.), *Explaining Emotions*. Berkeley: University of California Press: 223–50.

Greenspan, P. (1988) *Emotions and Reasons*. London: Routledge.

Griffiths, P. (1993) 'Functional analysis and proper functions', *British Journal for the Philosophy of Science* 44(3): 409–22.

Griffiths, P. (1997) *What Emotions Really Are*. Chicago: University of Chicago Press.

Gunther, Y. (2004) 'The phenomenology and intentionality of emotion', *Philosophical Studies* 117(1–2): 43–55.

Hamlyn, D.W. (1989) 'False emotions', *Proceedings of the Aristotelian Society*, Supp. Vol. 63: 275–86.

Hardcastle, V. (1999) 'Understanding functions: a pragmatic approach', in V. Hardcastle (ed.), *Where Biology Meets Psychology: Philosophical Essays*. Cambridge, MA: MIT Press: 27–43.

Haybron, D. (2008) *The Pursuit of Unhappiness*. Oxford: Oxford University Press.

Helm, B. (2001) *Emotional Reason: Deliberation, Motivation and the Nature of Value*. Cambridge: Cambridge University Press.

Helm, B. (2009) 'Emotions as evaluative feelings', *Emotion Review* 1(3): 248–55.

Hohmann, G. (1966) 'Some effects of spinal cord lesions on experienced emotional feelings', *Psychophysiology* 3(2): 143–56.

Hutcheson, F. (2002) [1728] *Essay on the Nature and Conduct of the Passions with Illustrations on the Moral Sense*, ed. A. Garrett. Indianapolis, IN: Liberty Fund.

James, W. (1884) 'What is an emotion?', *Mind* 9(2): 188–205.

James, W. (1890) *The Principles of Psychology*. New York: Dover.

Jefferson, M. (1983) 'What is wrong with sentimentality?', *Mind* 92(368): 519–29.

Johnson-Laird, P. and Oatley, K. (1992) 'Basic emotions, rationality and folk theory', *Cognition and Emotion* 6(3–4): 201–23.

Knight, D. (1999) 'Why we enjoy condemning sentimentality: a meta-aesthetic perspective', *Journal of Aesthetics and Art Criticism* 57: 411–20.

Kupfer, J. (1996) 'The sentimental self', *Canadian Journal of Philosophy* 26(4): 543–60.

Lange, C. (1922) [1885] 'The emotions: a psychophysical study', I.A. Haupt (trans.), in C.G. Lange and W. James (eds), *The Emotions*, Vol. 1. Baltimore: Williams and Wilkins: 33–90.

Lazarus, R. (1991) *Emotion and Adaptation*. Oxford: Oxford University Press.

Lyons, W. (1980) *Emotion*. Cambridge: Cambridge University Press.

Marino, P. (2010) 'Moral rationalism and the normative status of desiderative coherence', *Journal of Moral Philosophy* 7(2): 227–52.

Marks, J. (1982) 'A theory of emotion', *Philosophical Studies* 42(1): 227–42.

Millgram, E. (1993) 'Pleasure in practical reasoning', *Monist* 76(3): 394–415.

Milligan, T. (2008) 'False emotions', *Philosophy* 83(324): 213–30.

Millikan, R. (1984) *Language, Thought and Other Biological Categories*. Cambridge, MA: MIT Press.

Millikan, R. (1989). 'In defense of proper functions', *Philosophy of Science* 56: 288–302.

Millikan, R. (1995) 'Pushmi-pullyu representations', *Philosophical Perspectives* 9: 185–200.

Montague, M. (2009) 'The logic, intentionality, and phenomenology of emotion', *Philosophical Studies* 145(2): 171–92.

Morton, A. (2010) 'Epistemic emotions', in P. Goldie (ed.), *The Oxford Handbook of Philosophy of Emotion*. Oxford: Oxford University Press: 385–99.

Nash, R. (1989) 'Cognitive theories of emotion', *Noûs* 23(4): 481–504.

Neander, K. (1991) 'Functions as selected effects: the conceptual analyst's defense', *Philosophy of Science* 58: 168–84.

Neander, K. (1995) 'Misrepresenting and malfunctioning', *Philosophical Studies* 79: 109–41.

Neander, K. (2012) 'Teleological theories of mental content', in *The Stanford Encyclopedia of Philosophy* (Spring Edition), ed. E. Zalta: http://plato.stanford.edu/archives/spr2012/entries/content-teleological/.

Newman, I. (2002) 'On the alleged unwholesomeness of sentimentality', in A. Neill and A. Ridley (eds), *Arguing About Art*, second edition. London: Routledge: 320–32.

Nussbaum, M. (2001) *Upheavals of Thought: The Intelligence of Emotions*. Cambridge: Cambridge University Press.

Parfit, D. (1984) *Reasons and Persons*. Oxford: Oxford University Press.

Percival, P. (1992) 'Thank goodness that's non-actual', *Philosophical Papers* 21(3): 191–213.

Price, C. (2001) *Functions in Mind: A Theory of Intentional Content*. Oxford: Oxford University Press.

Price, C. (2006a) 'Fearing Fluffy: the content of an emotional appraisal', in G. MacDonald and D. Papineau (eds), *Teleosemantics*. Oxford: Oxford University Press: 208–28.

Price, C. (2006b) 'Affect without object: moods and objectless emotions', *European Journal of Analytic Philosophy* 2(1): 49–68.

Price, C. (2010) 'The rationality of grief', *Inquiry* 53(1): 20–40.

Price, C. (2012a) 'What is the point of love?', *International Journal of Philosophical Studies* 20(2): 217–37.

Price, C. (2012b) 'Doing without emotions', *Pacific Philosophical Quarterly* 93(3): 317–37.

Price, C. (2013) 'The problem of emotional significance', *Acta Analytica* 28(2): 189–206.

Prinz, J. (2004) *Gut Reactions: A Perceptual Theory of Emotion*. Oxford: Oxford University Press.

Prinz, J. (2008) 'Is emotion a form of perception?', in L. Faucher and C. Tappolet (eds), *The Modularity of Emotions*. Calgary: University of Calgary Press: 137–60.

Pugmire, D (1994) 'Real emotion', *Philosophy and Phenomenological Research* 54(1): 105–22.

Pugmire, D. (2005) *Sound Sentiments: Integrity in the Emotions*. Oxford: Oxford University Press.

Roberts, R. (1988) 'What an emotion is: a sketch', *The Philosophical Review* 97: 183–209.

Roberts, R. (2003) *Emotions: An Essay in Aid of Moral Psychology*. Cambridge: Cambridge University Press.

Robinson, J. (2005) *Deeper than Reason: Emotion and Its Role in Literature, Music and Art*. Oxford: Oxford University Press.

Rorty, A. (1980) 'Introduction', in A. Rorty (ed.), *Explaining Emotions*. Berkeley and Los Angeles: University of California Press: 1–8.

Rorty, A. (2010) 'A plea for ambivalence', in P. Goldie (ed.), *The Oxford Handbook of Philosophy of Emotion*. Oxford: Oxford University Press: 425–44.

Rozin, P., Millman, L. and Nemeroff, C. (1986) 'Operation of the laws of sympathetic magic in disgust and other domains', *Journal of Personality and Social Psychology* 50(4): 703–12.

Sabini, J. and Silver, M. (2005) 'Why emotion names and experiences don't neatly pair', *Psychological Inquiry* 16(1): 11–48.

Savile, A. (1982) *The Test of Time*. Oxford: Clarendon Press.

Scanlon, T. (1998) *What Do We Owe to Each Other?* Cambridge, MA: Belknap Press.

Schlosser, G. (1998) 'Self-reproduction and functionality: a systems-theoretical approach to teleological explanation', *Synthese* 116(3): 303–54.

Shaffer, J. (1983) 'An assessment of emotion', *American Philosophical Quarterly* 20(2): 161–73.

Solomon, R. (1973) 'Emotions and choice', *The Review of Metaphysics* 27(1): 20–41.

Solomon, R. (1993) [1976] *The Passions: Emotions and the Meaning of Life*. Indianapolis, IN: Hackett.

Solomon, R. (2003a) [1988] 'On emotions as judgments', in *Not Passion's Slave*. Oxford: Oxford University Press: 92–113.

Solomon, R. (2003b) 'What is a "cognitive theory of the emotions", and does it neglect affectivity?', in *Not Passion's Slave*. Oxford: Oxford University Press: 178–94.

Solomon, R. (2003c) 'On the passivity of the passions', in *Not Passion's Slave*. Oxford: Oxford University Press: 195–232.

Solomon, R. (ed.) (2003d) *What Is an Emotion? Classic and Contemporary Readings*. New York: Oxford.

Solomon, R. (2004) 'In defence of sentimentality', in *In Defence of Sentimentality*. Oxford: Oxford University Press: 3–19.

Solomon, R. (2007) *True to Our Feelings: What Our Emotions Are Really Telling Us*. Oxford: Oxford University Press.

Sterelny, K. (1990) *The Representational Theory of Mind: An Introduction*. Oxford: Blackwell.

Tanner, M. (1976) 'Sentimentality', *Proceedings of the Aristotelian Society* 77: 127–47.

Tappolet, C. (2002) 'Long-term emotions and emotional experiences in the explanation of actions', *European Review of Philosophy* 5: 151–61.

Tappolet, C. (2005) 'Ambivalent emotions and the perceptual account of emotions', *Analysis* 65(3): 229–33.

Tappolet, C. (2010) 'Emotion, motivation and action: the case of fear', in P. Goldie (ed.), *The Oxford Handbook of Philosophy of Emotion*. Oxford: Oxford University Press: 325–45.

Tappolet, C. (2012) 'Emotion, perception and emotional illusions', in C. Calabi (ed.), *Perceptual Illusions: Philosophical and Psychological Essays*. London: Palgrave-Macmillan: 205–22.

Taylor, G. (1985) *Pride, Shame, and Guilt*. Oxford: Oxford University Press.

Tooby, J. and Cosmides, L. (1990) 'The past explains the present: emotional adaptations and the structure of ancestral environments', *Ethology and Sociobiology* 11: 375–424.

Whiting, D. (2011) 'The feeling theory of emotion and the object-directed emotions', *European Journal of Philosophy* 19(2): 281–303.

Wright, L. (1976) *Teleological Explanations*. Berkeley and Los Angeles: University of California Press.

Index